# The
# Channeled Path
# to
# Immortality

by

Duane Lacoursiere and Morgan Gowans

RoseDog Books
PITTSBURGH, PENNSYLVANIA 15238

RoseDog Books
585 Alpha Drive
Pittsburgh, PA 15238
Visit our website at *www.rosedogbookstore.com*

ISBN: 979-8-89027-255-3
eISBN: 979-8-89027-753-4

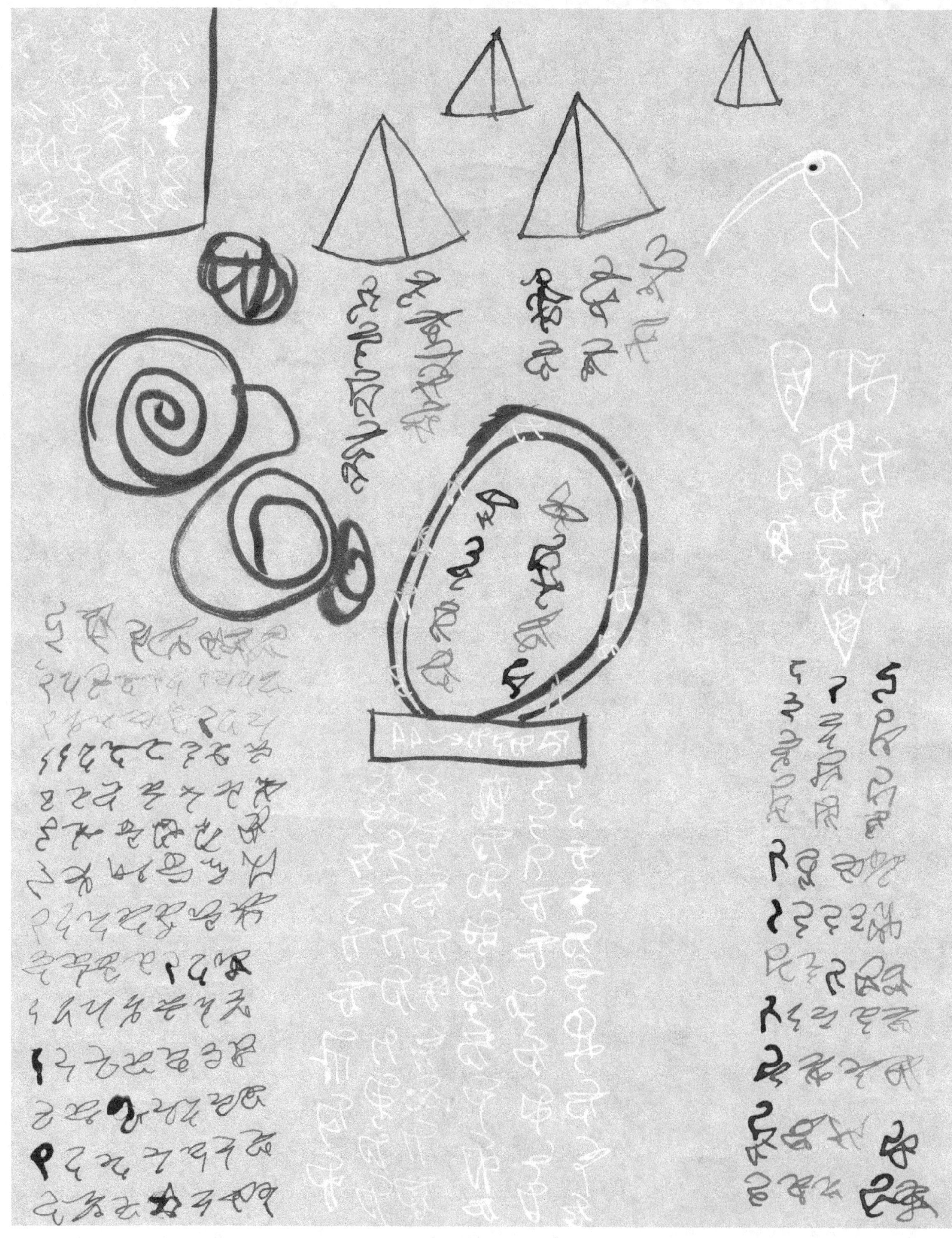

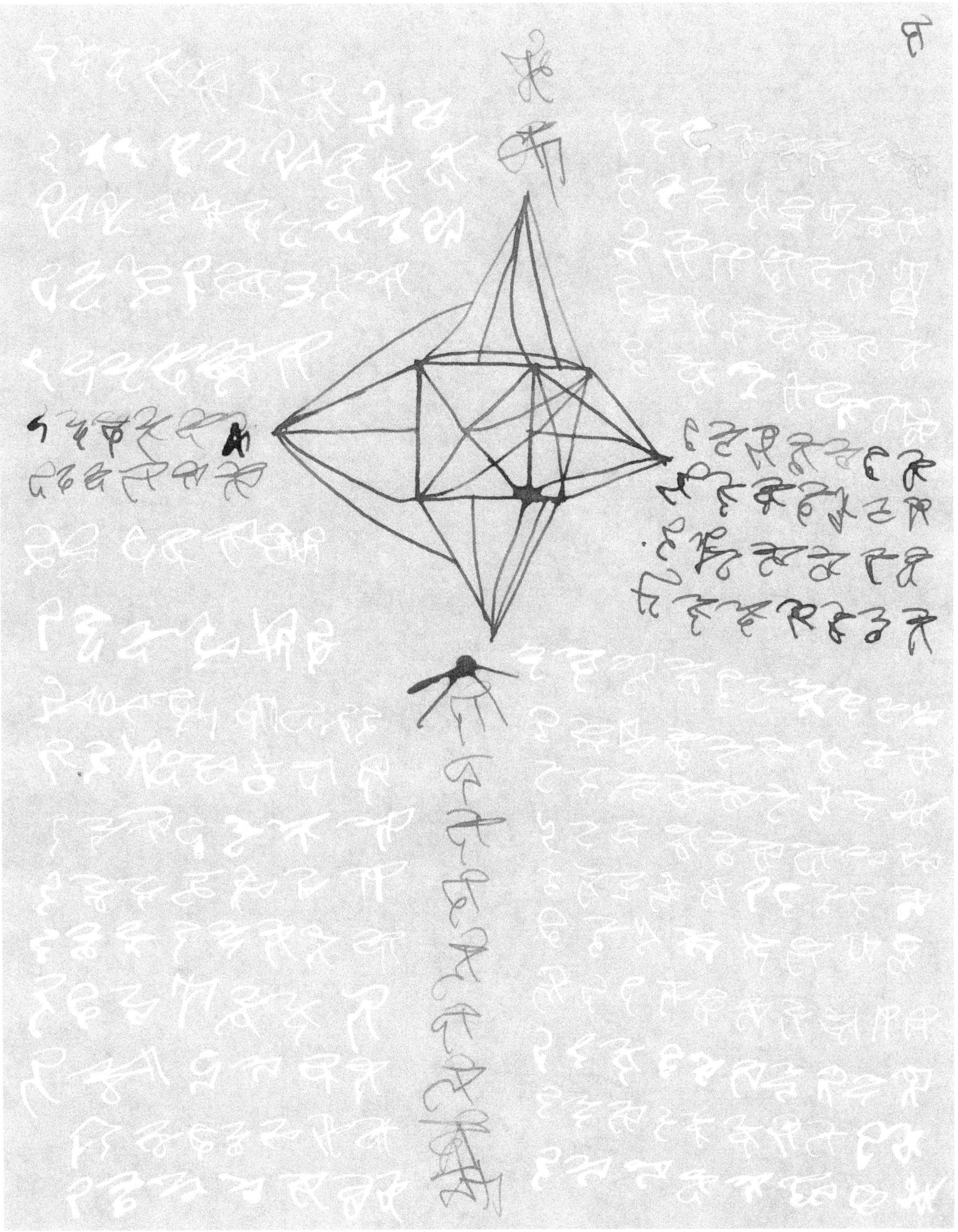

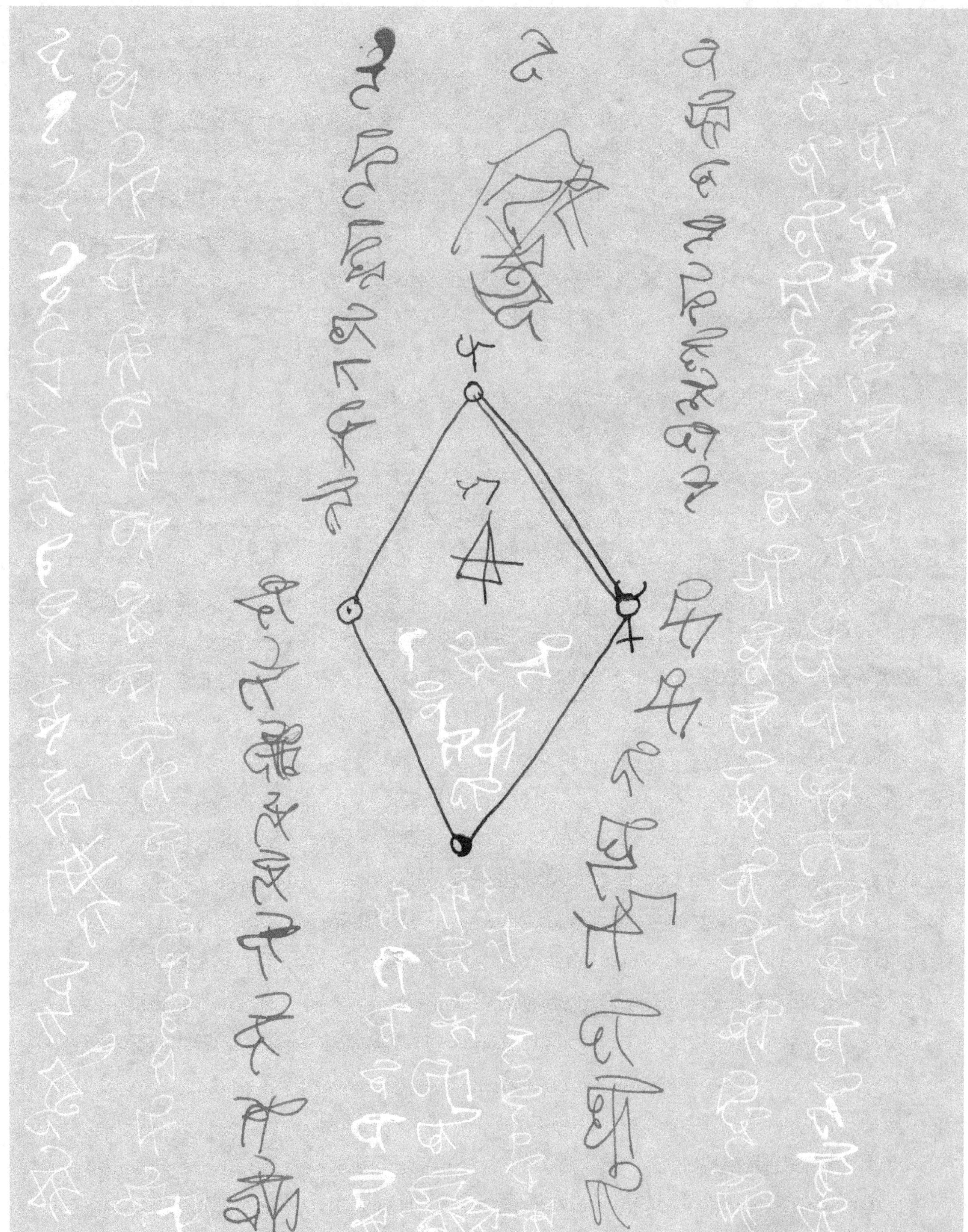

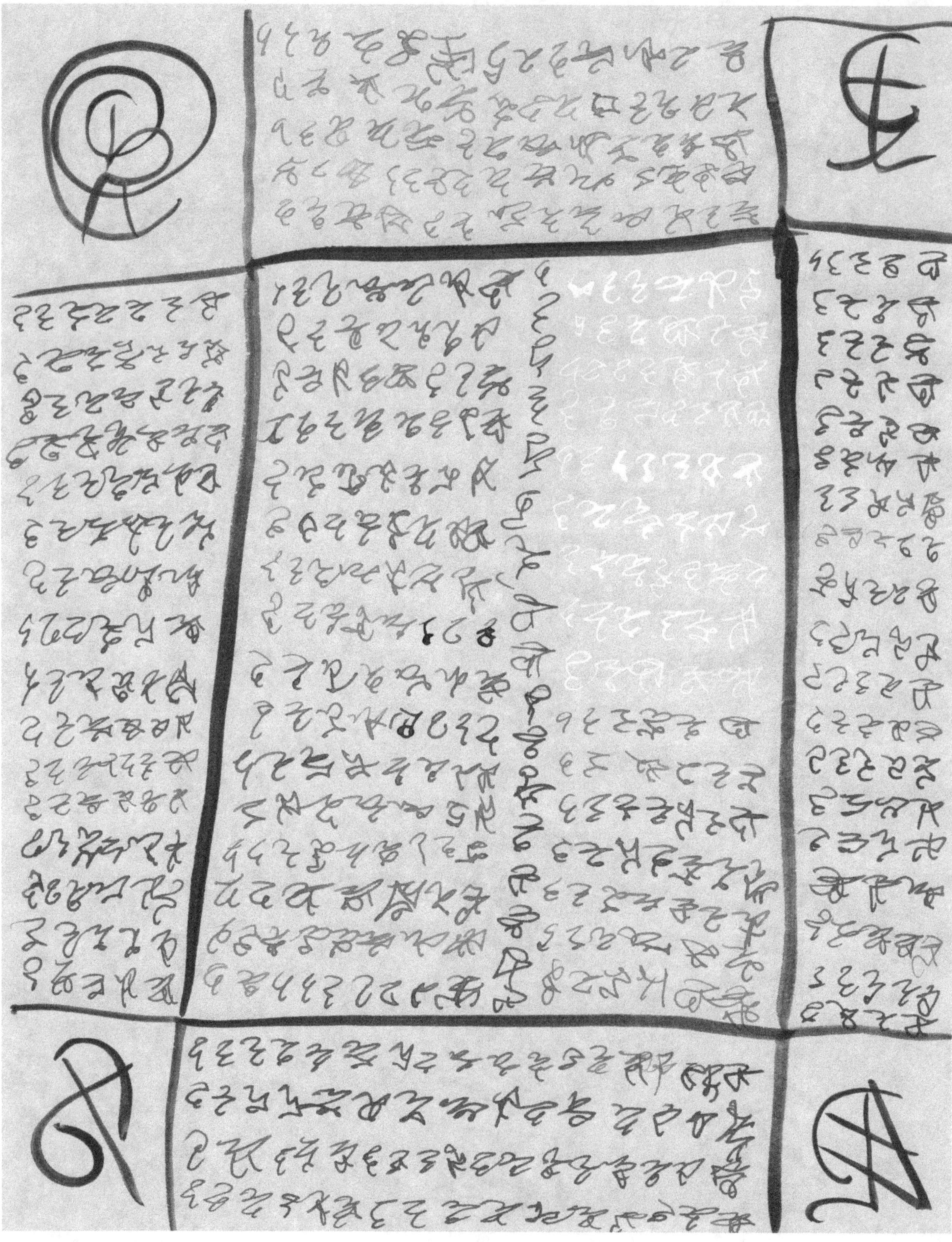

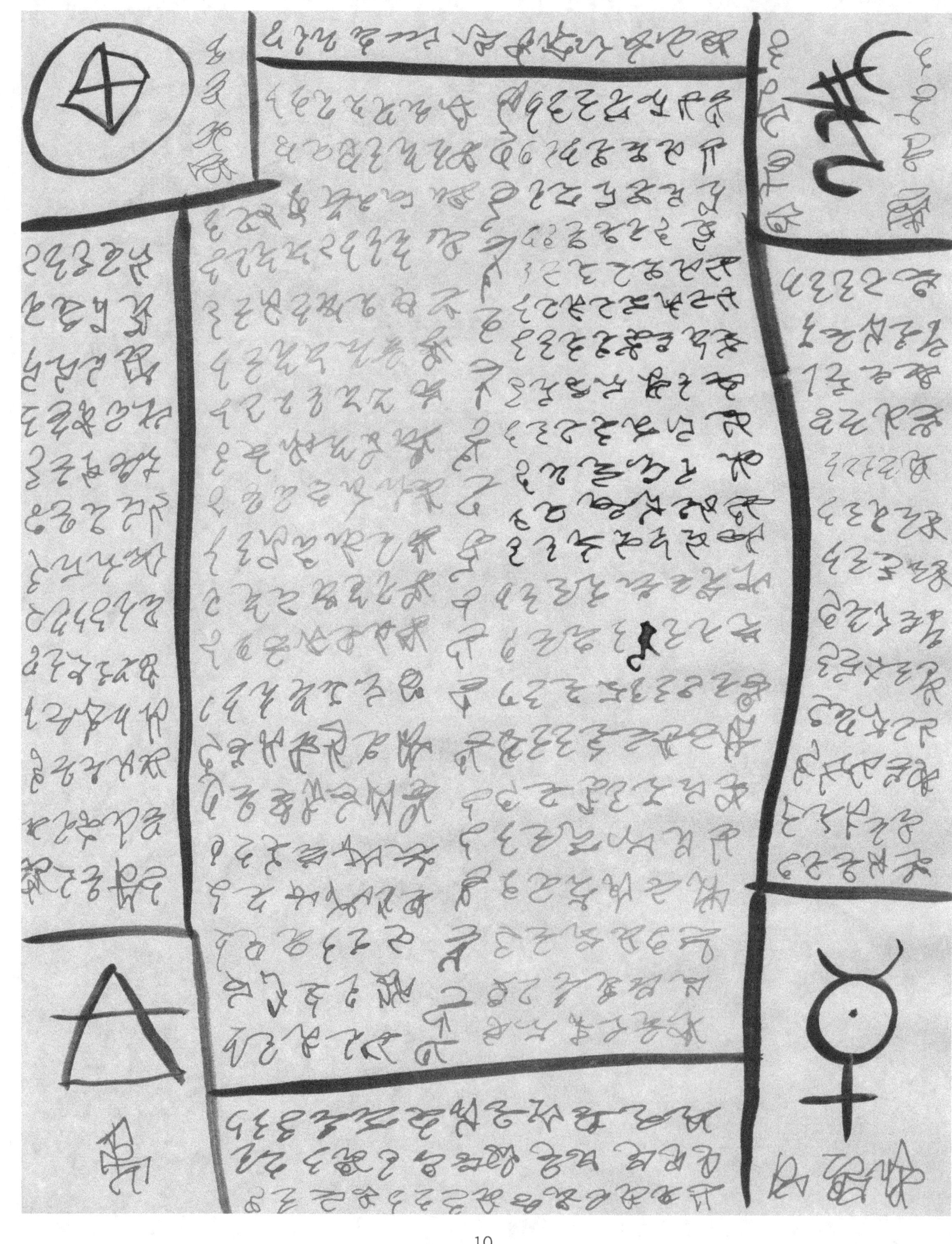

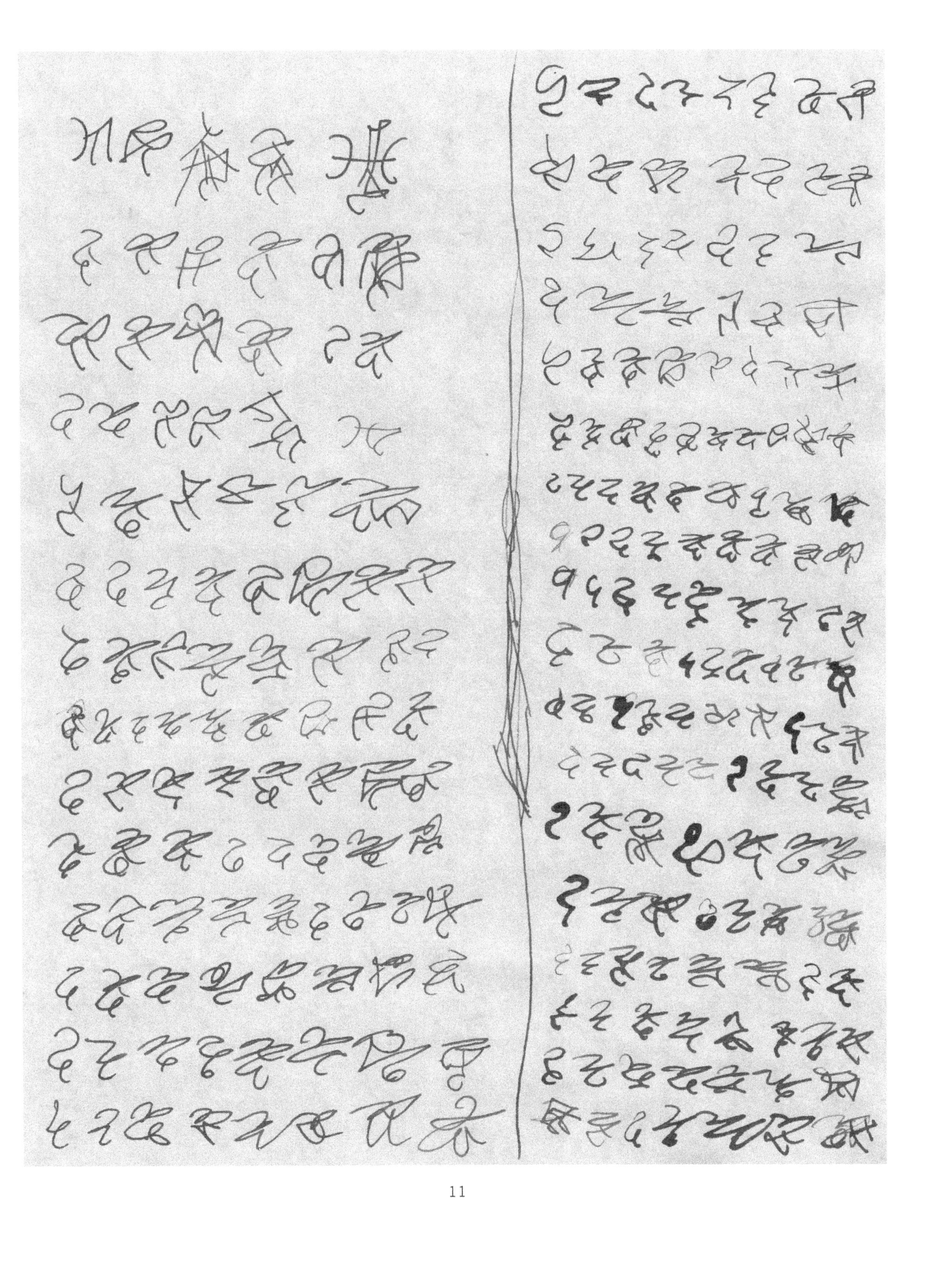

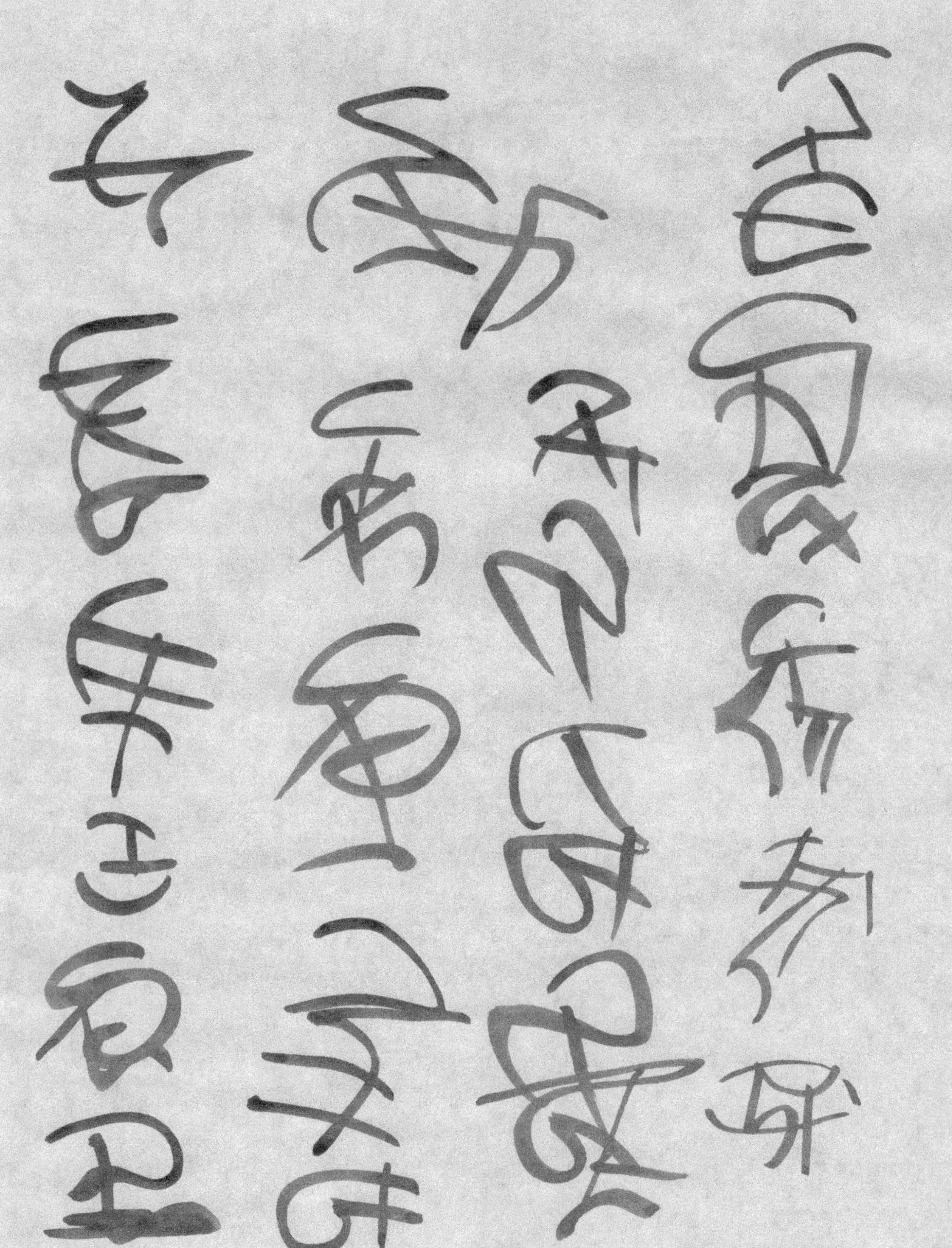

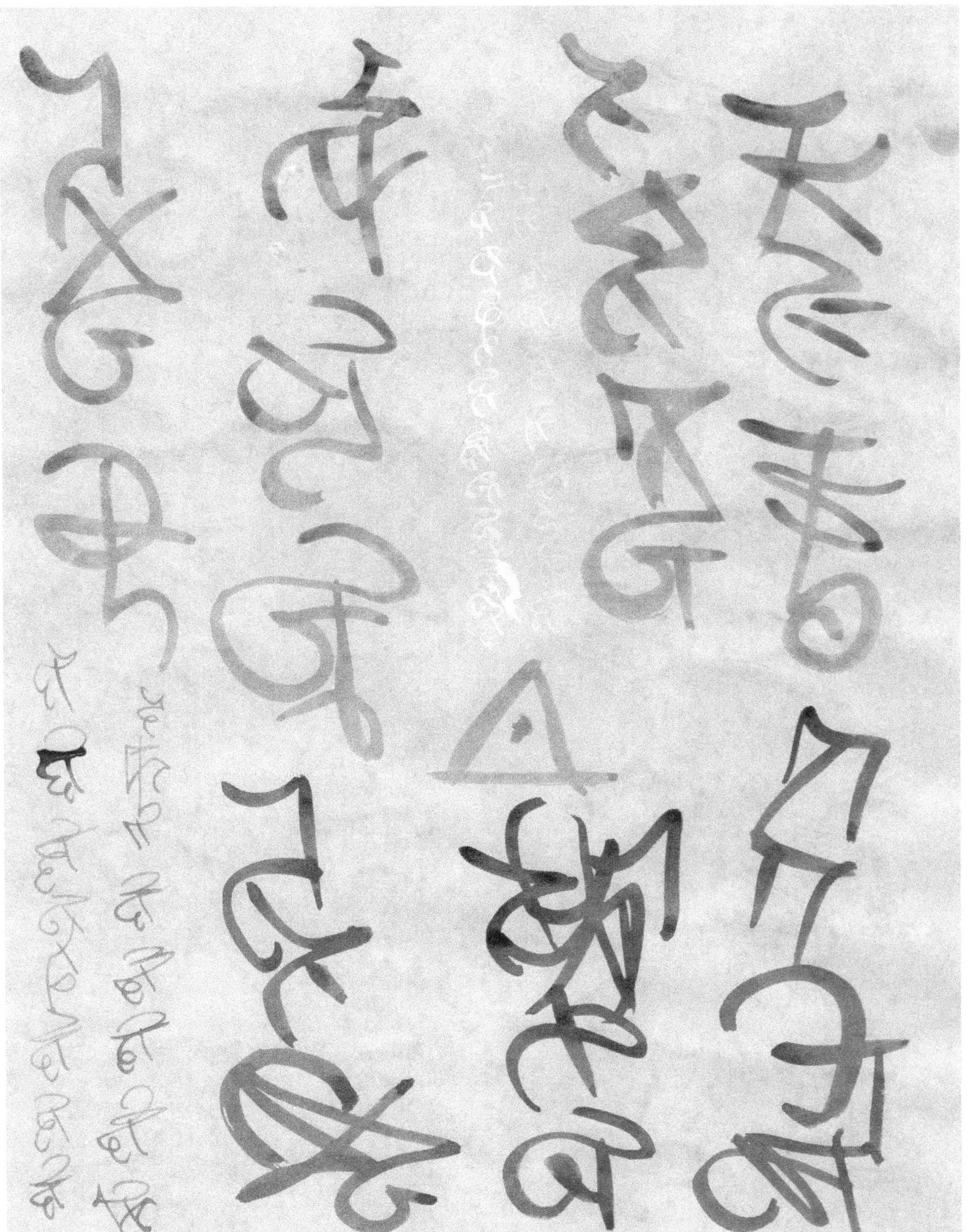

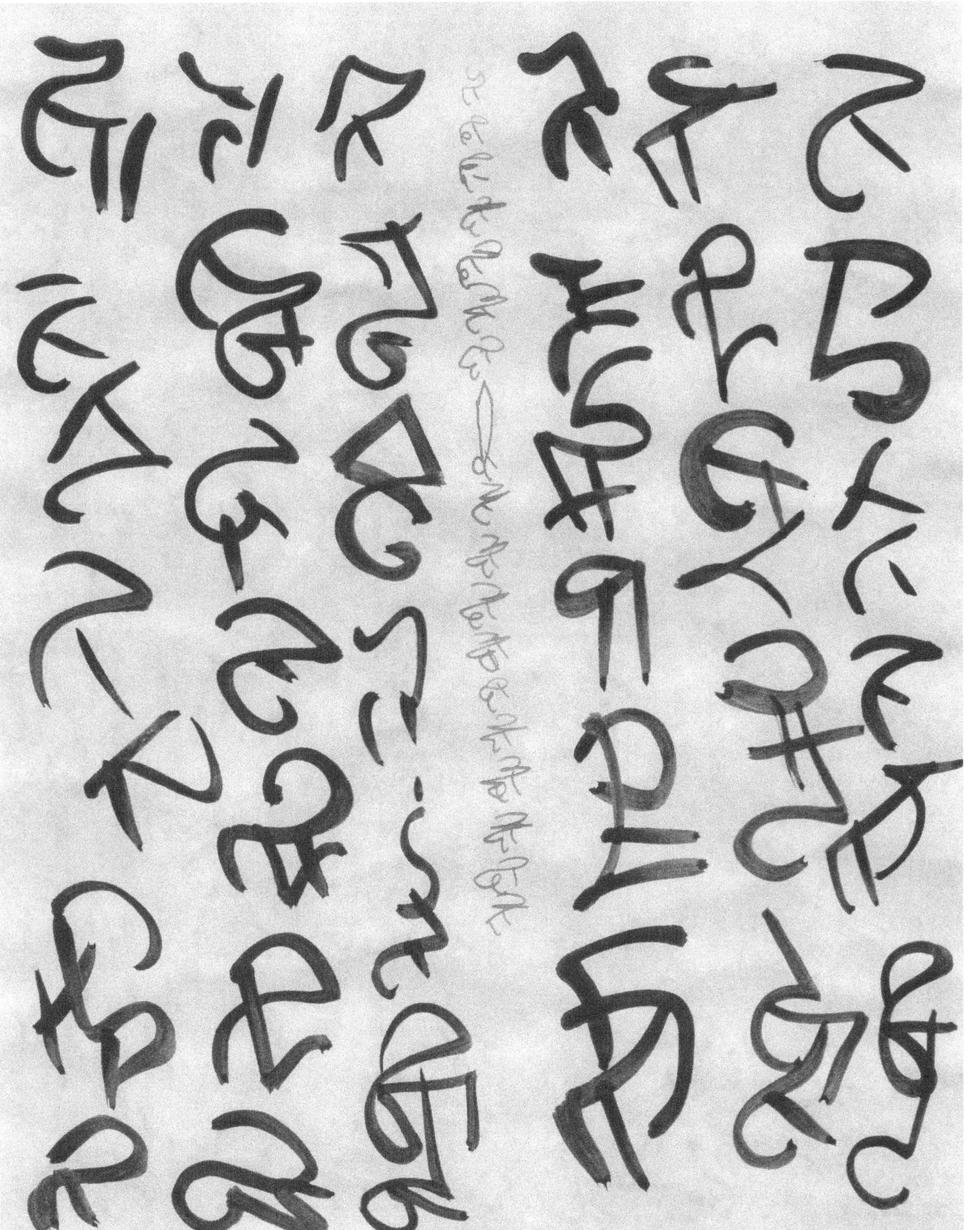

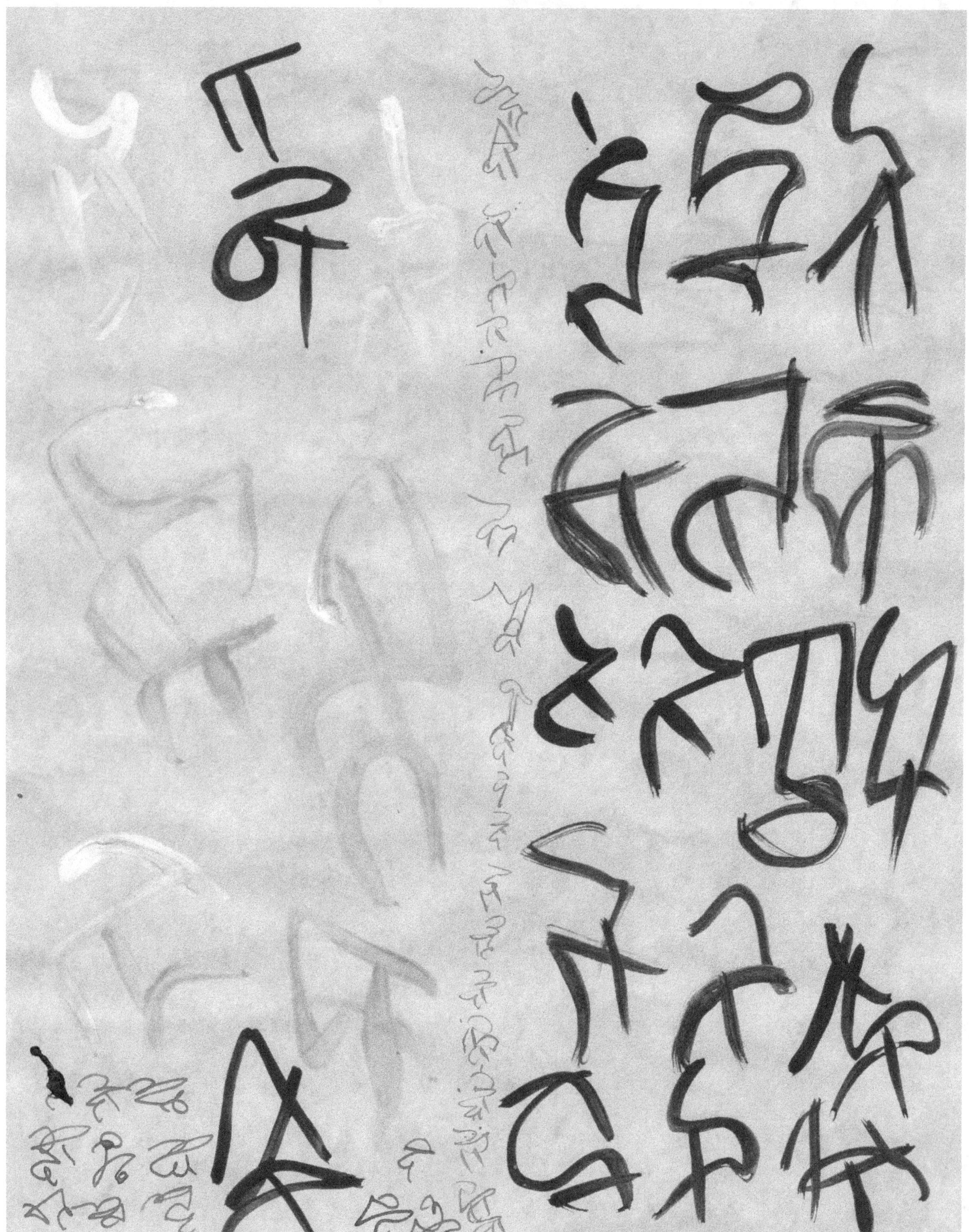

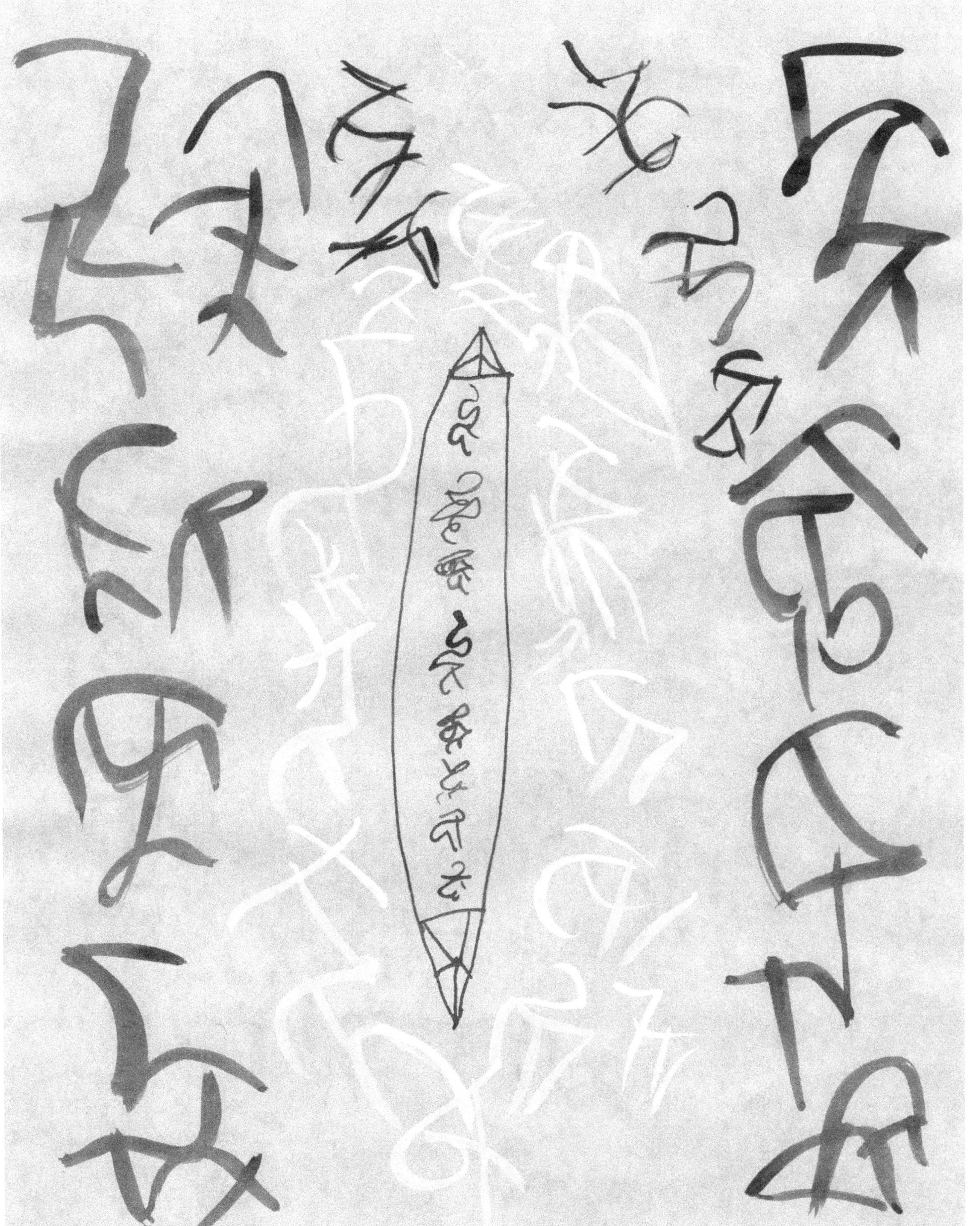

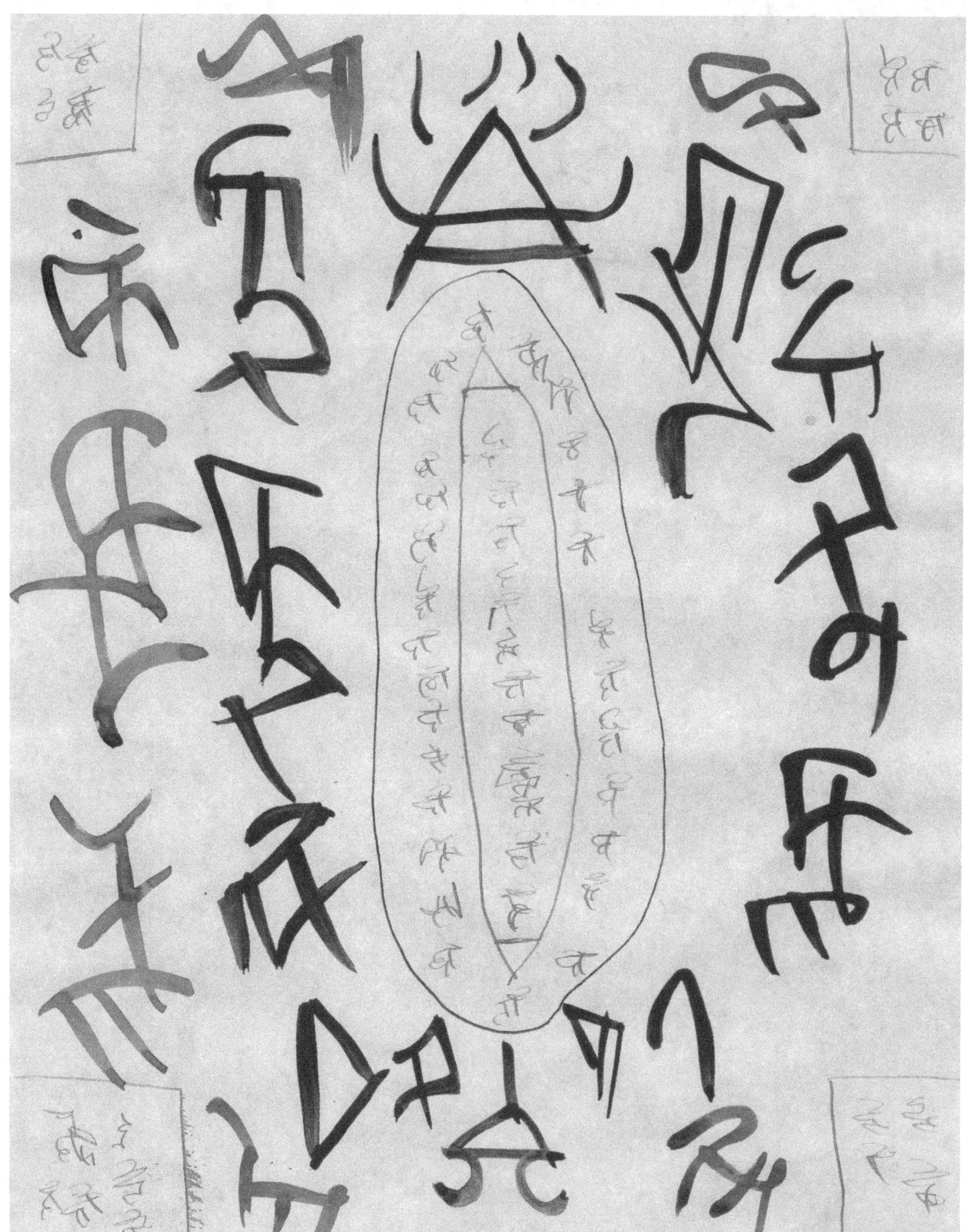

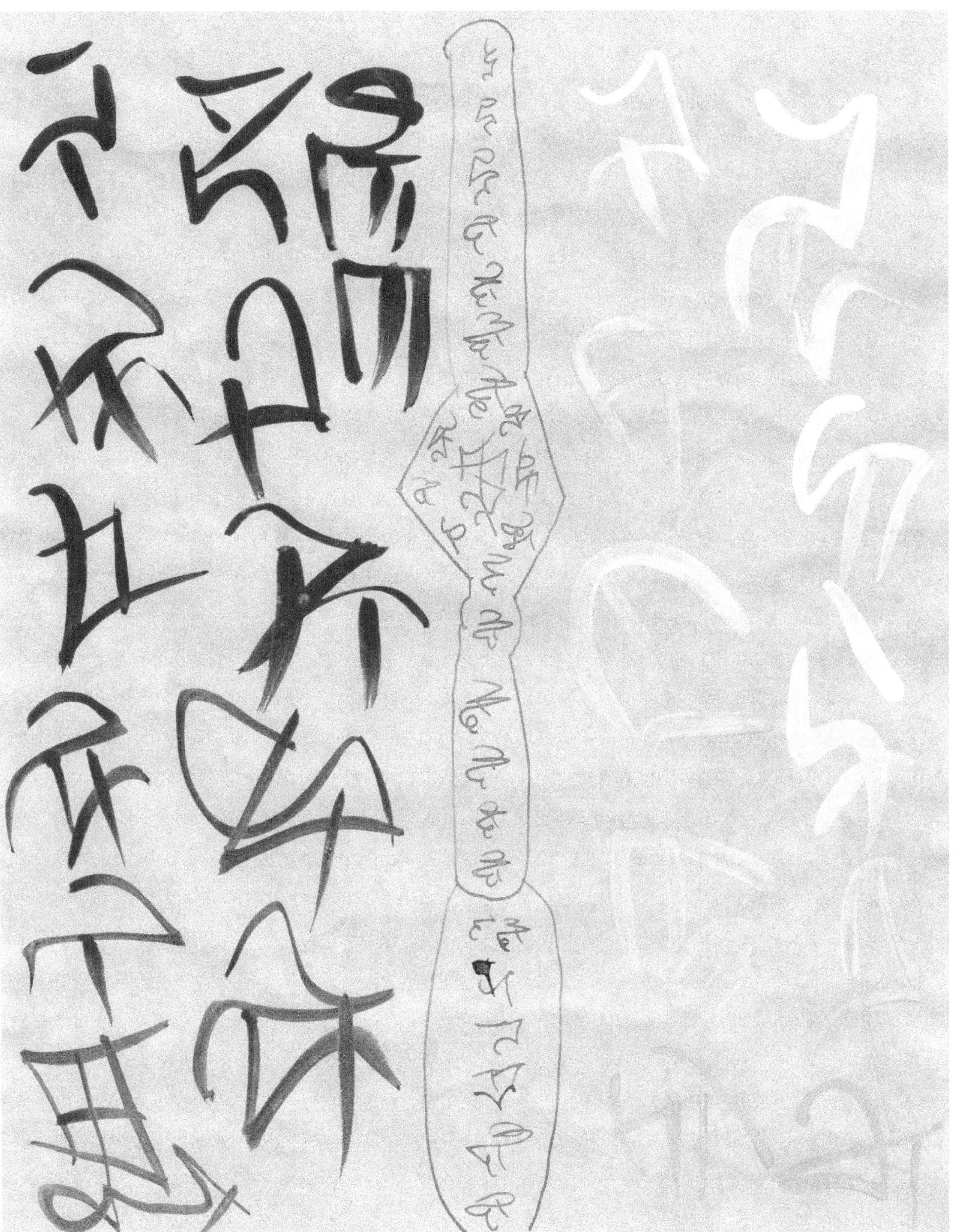

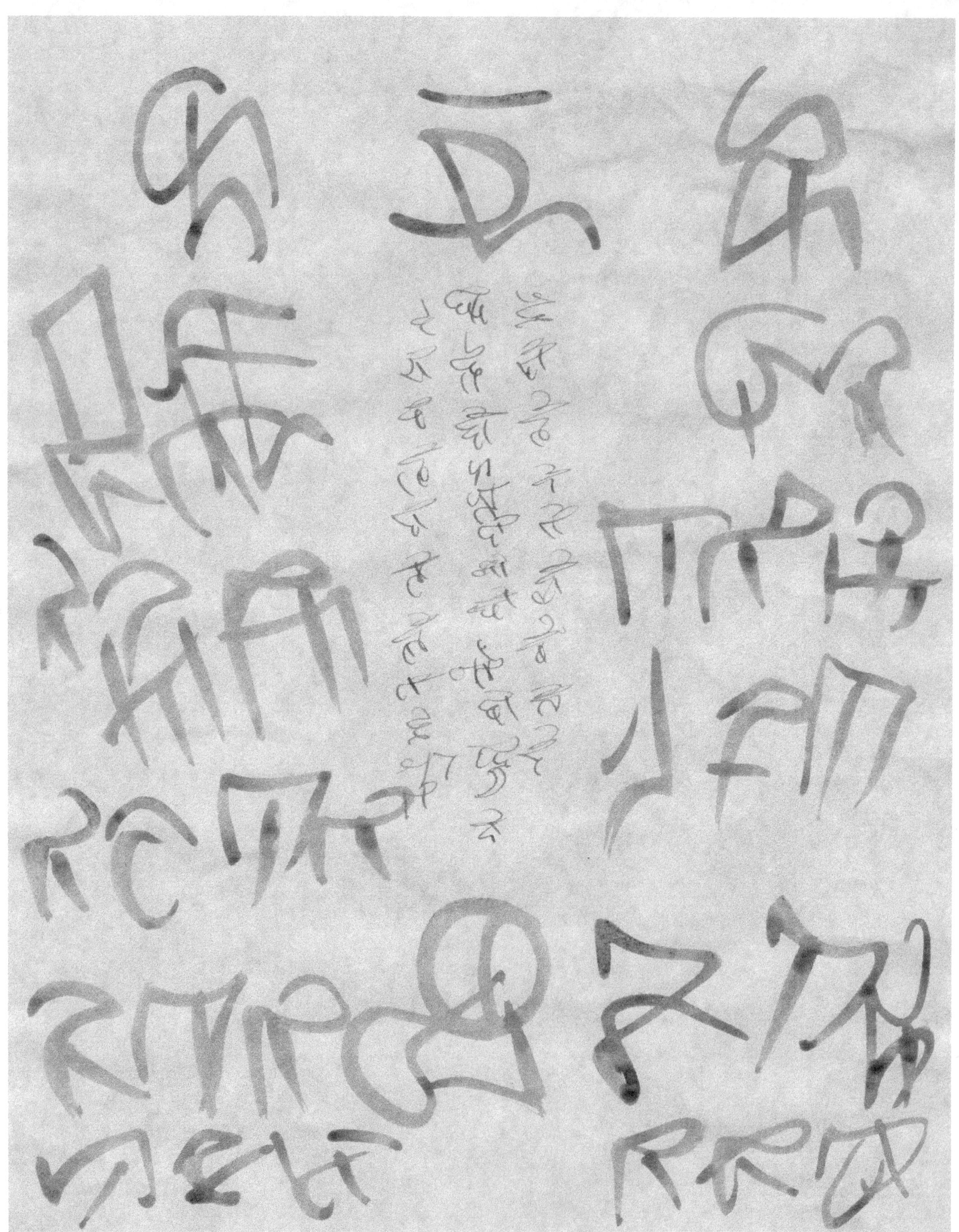

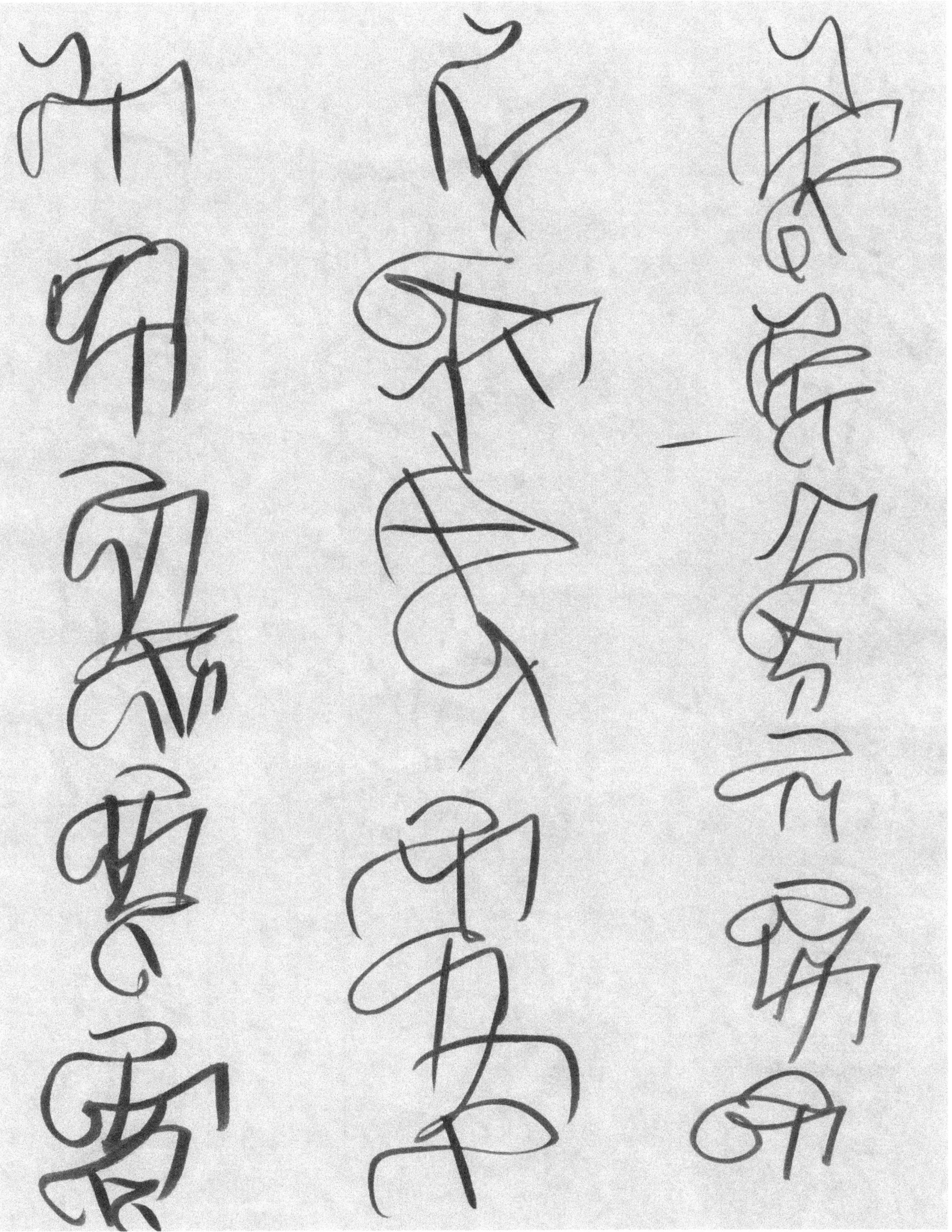

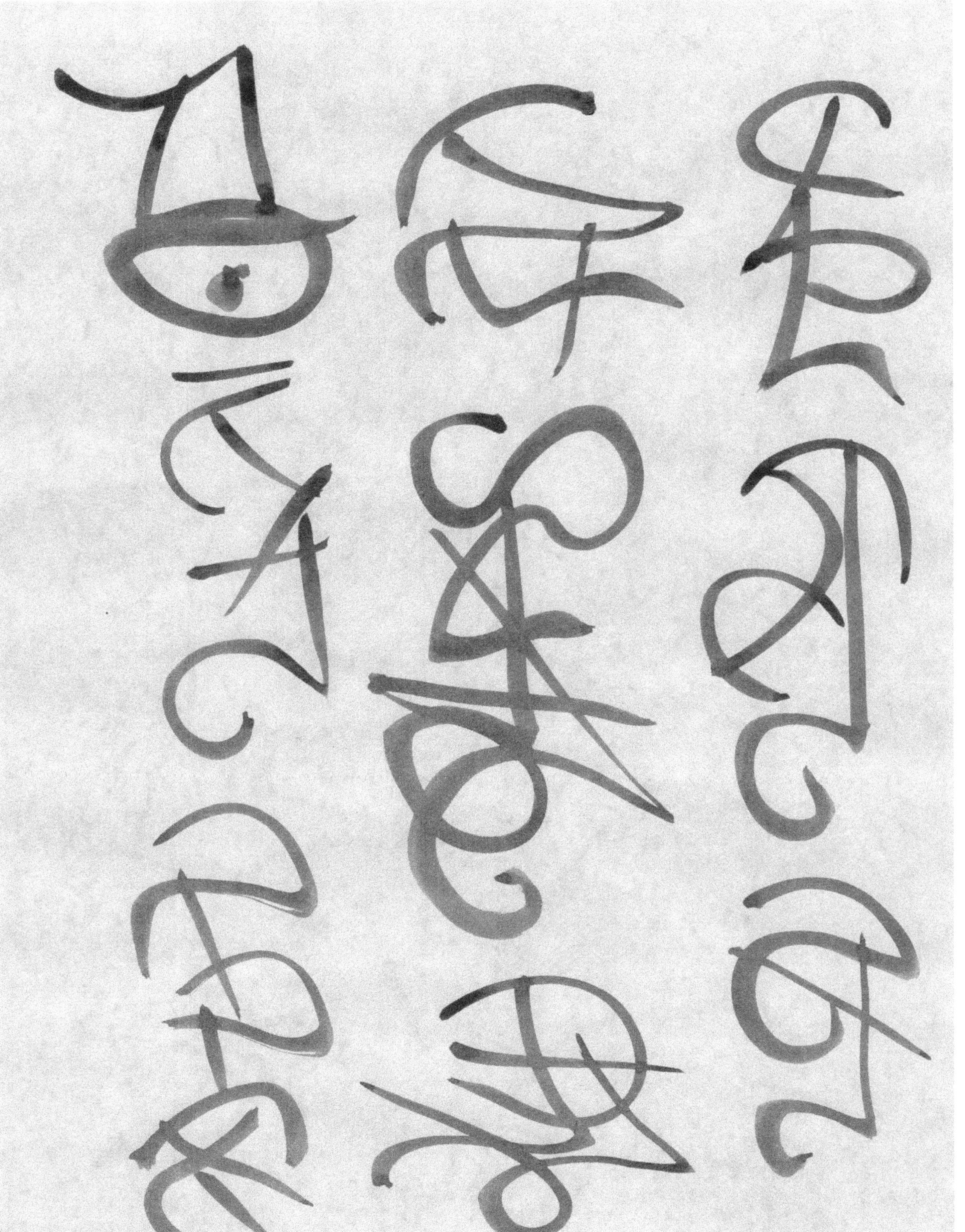

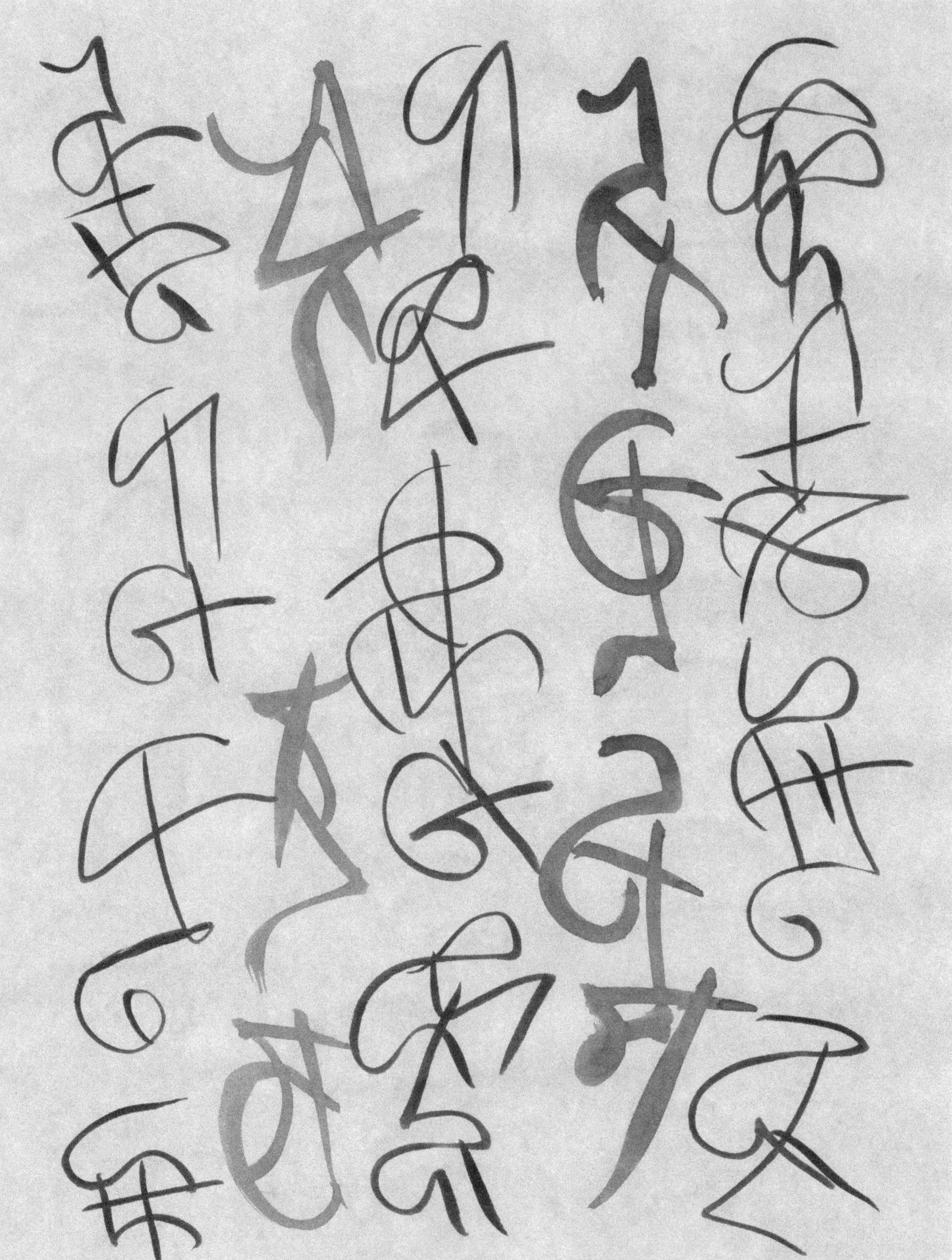

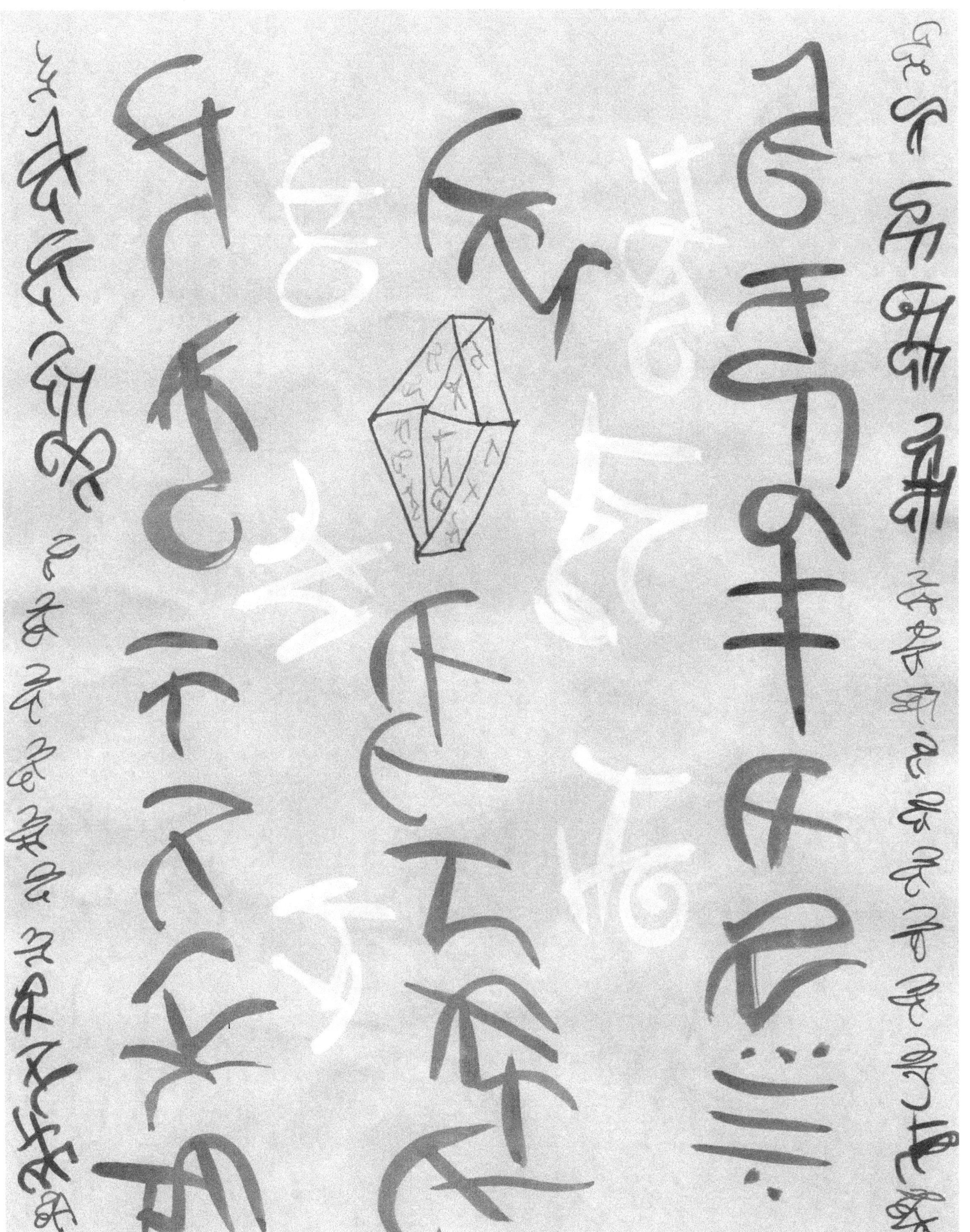

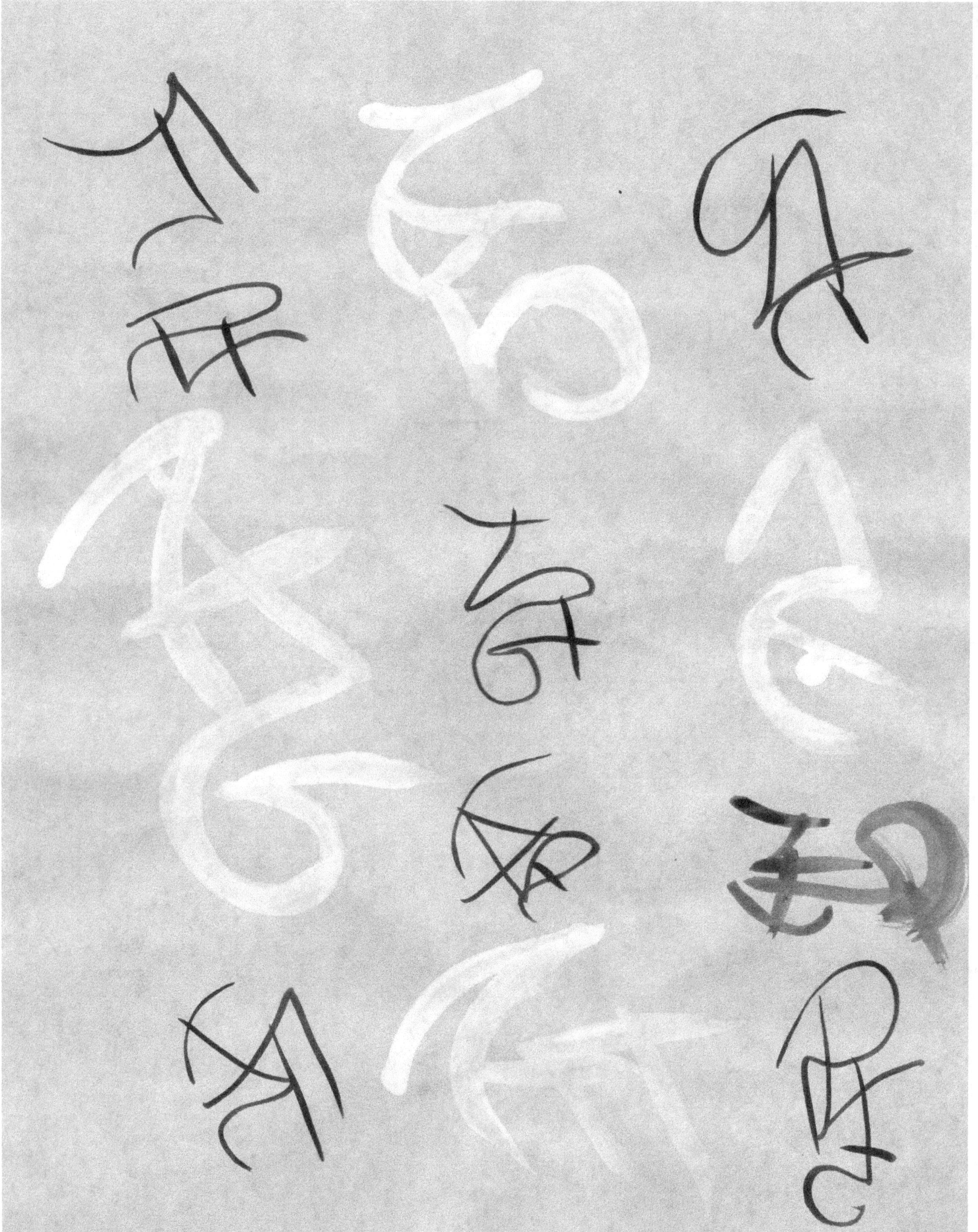

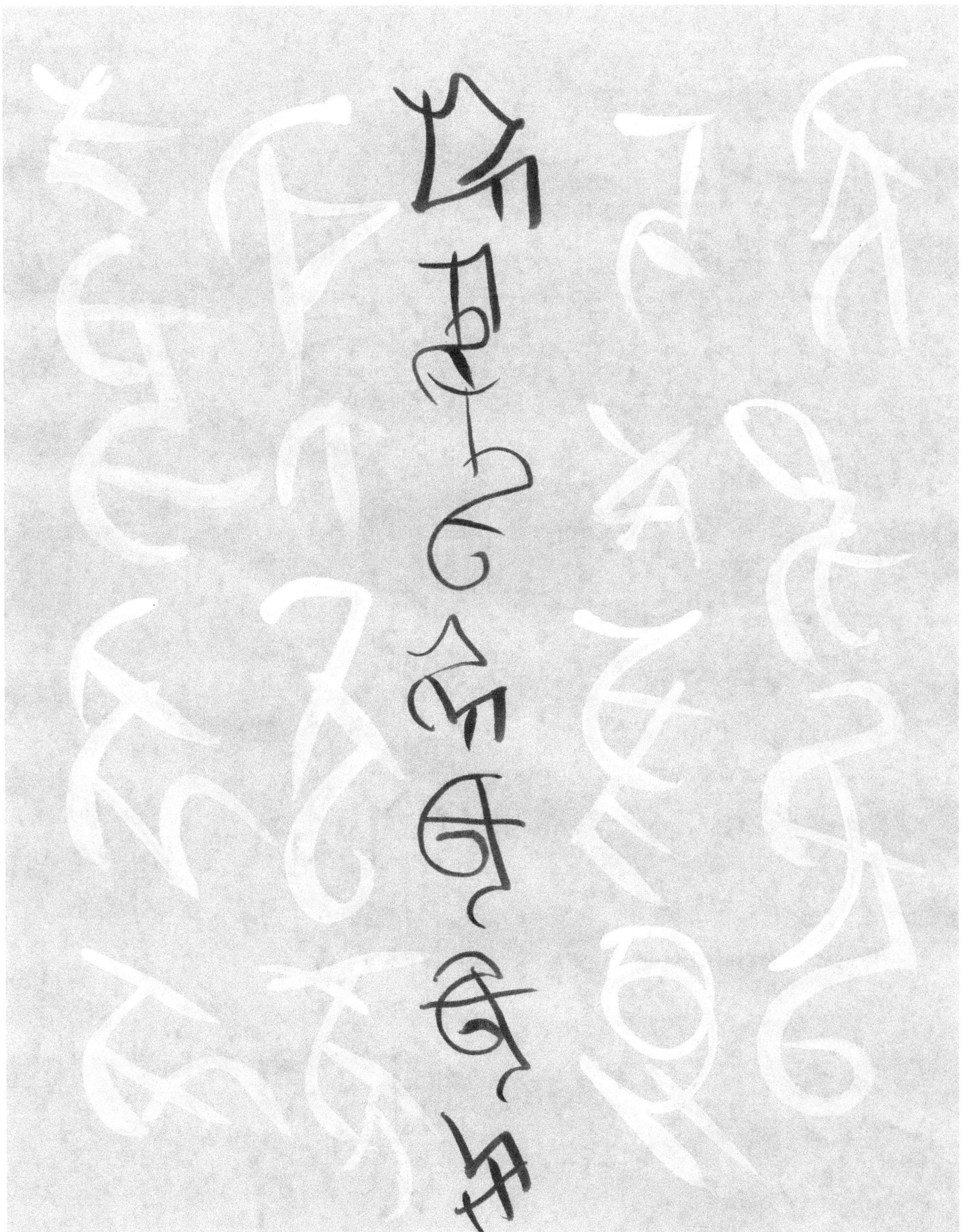

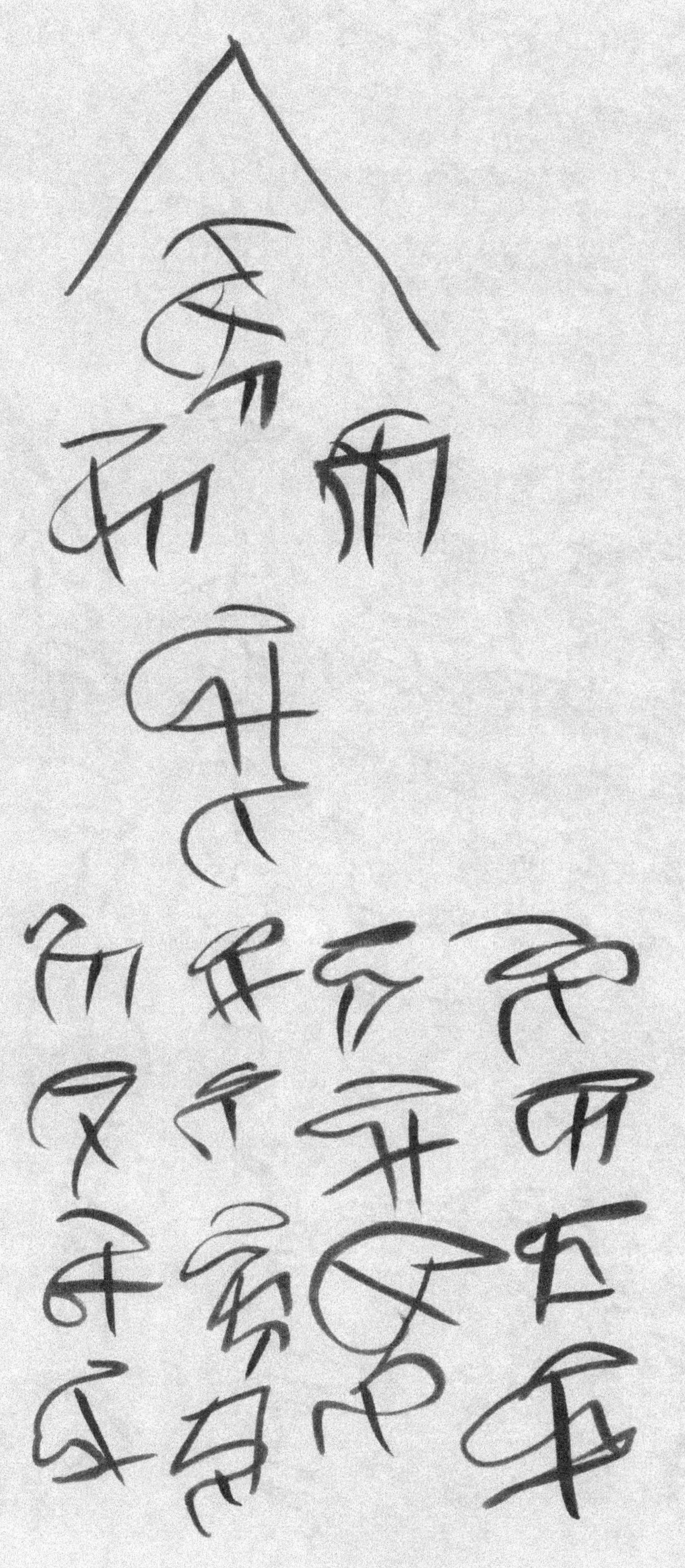

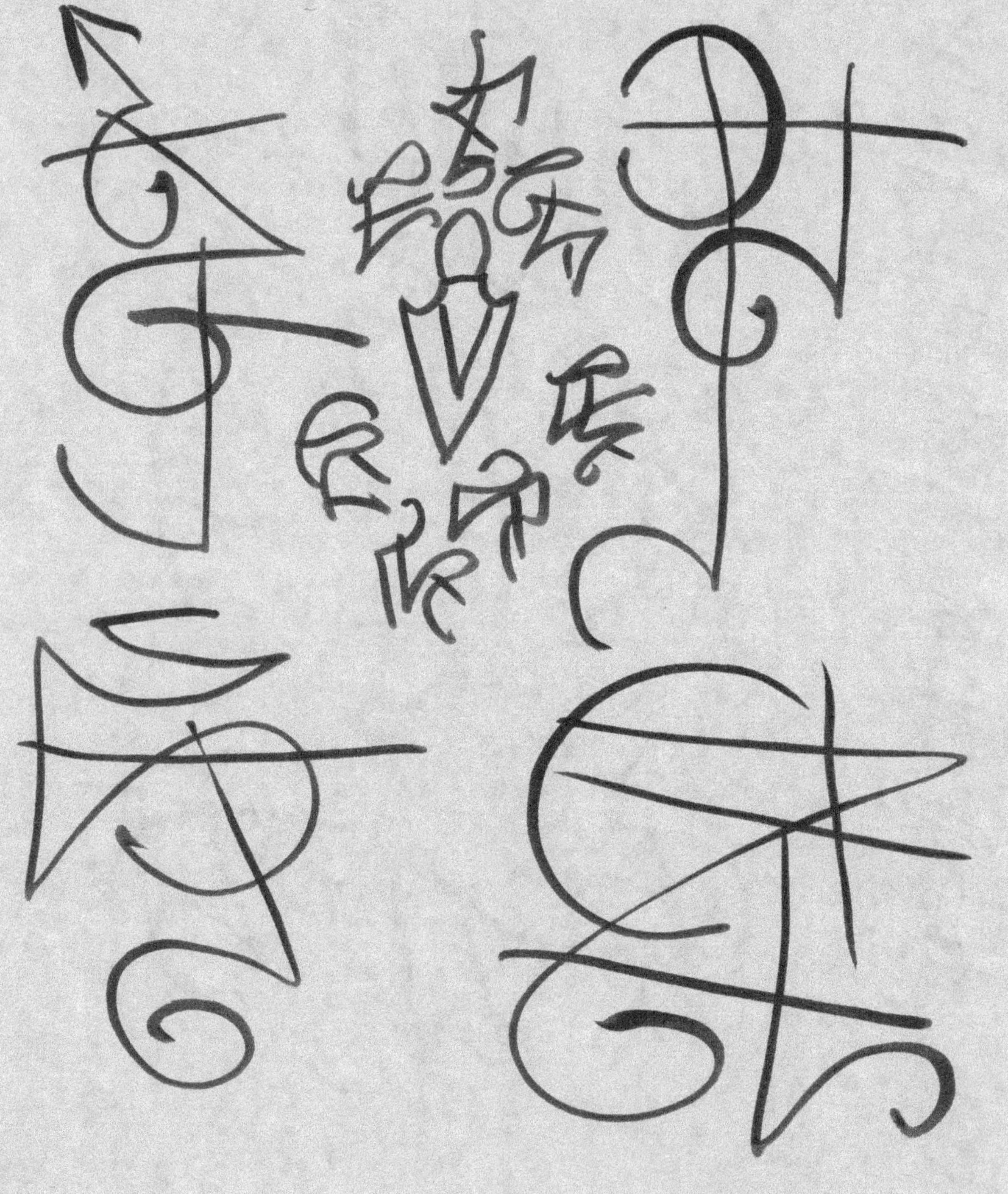

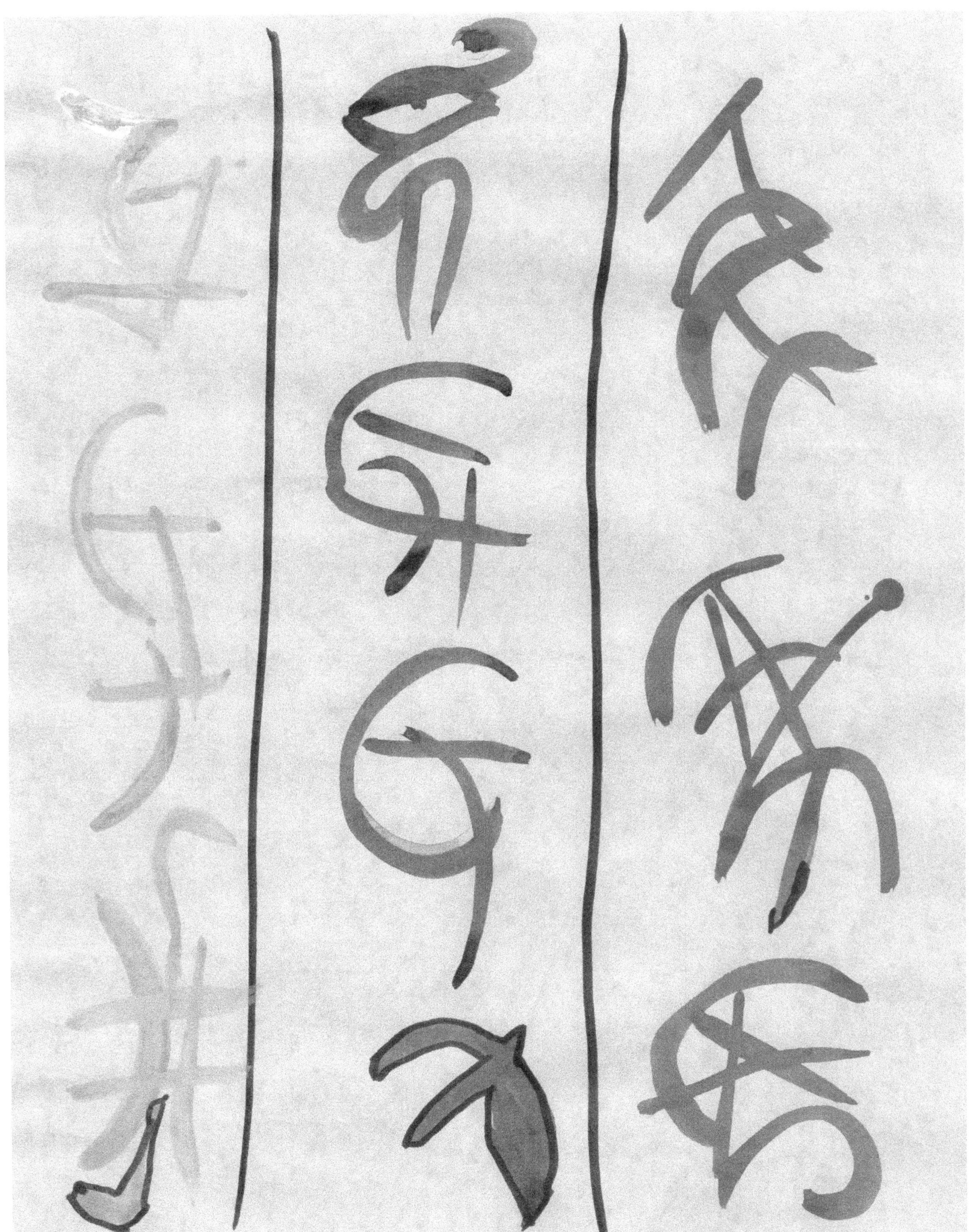

[illegible]

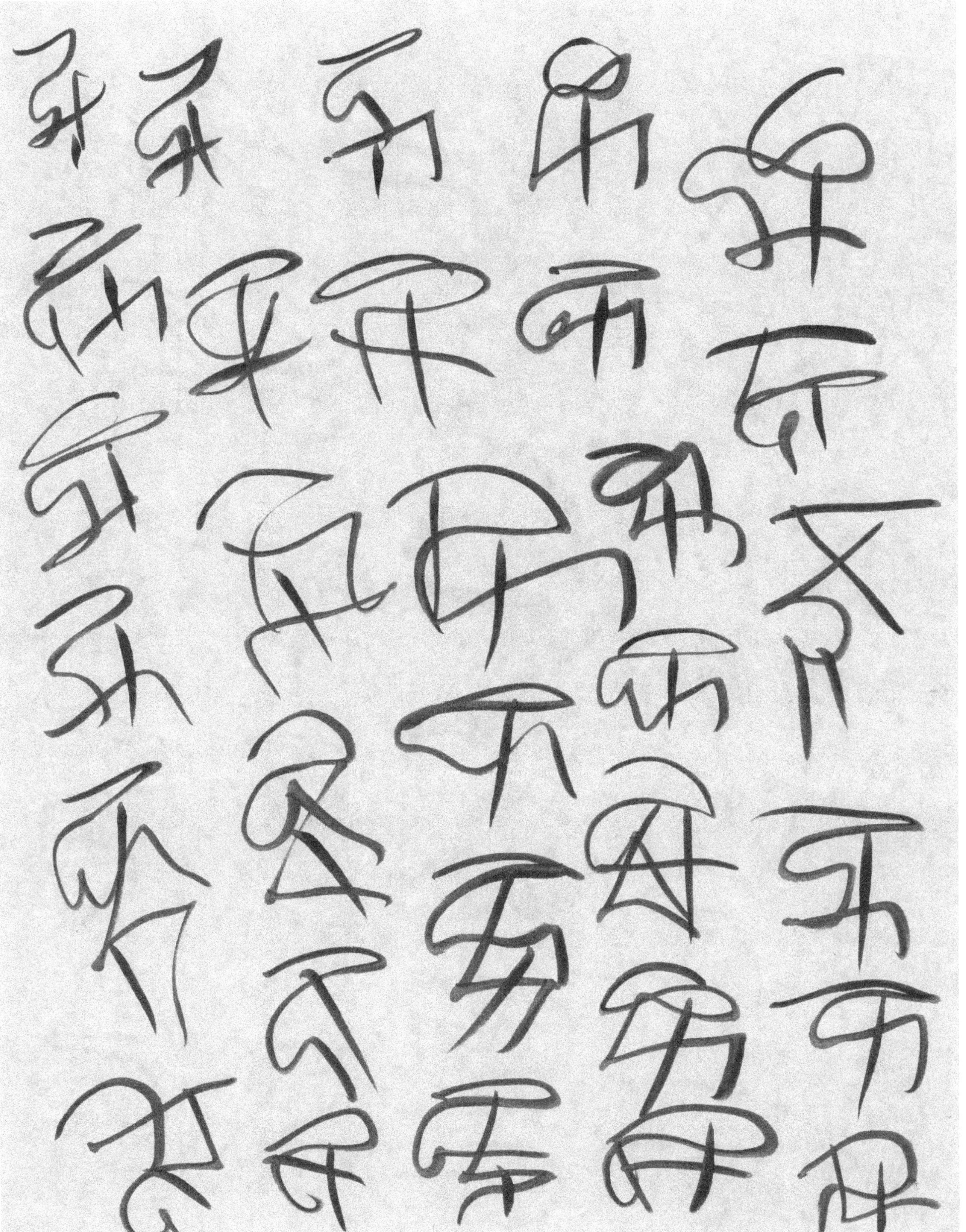

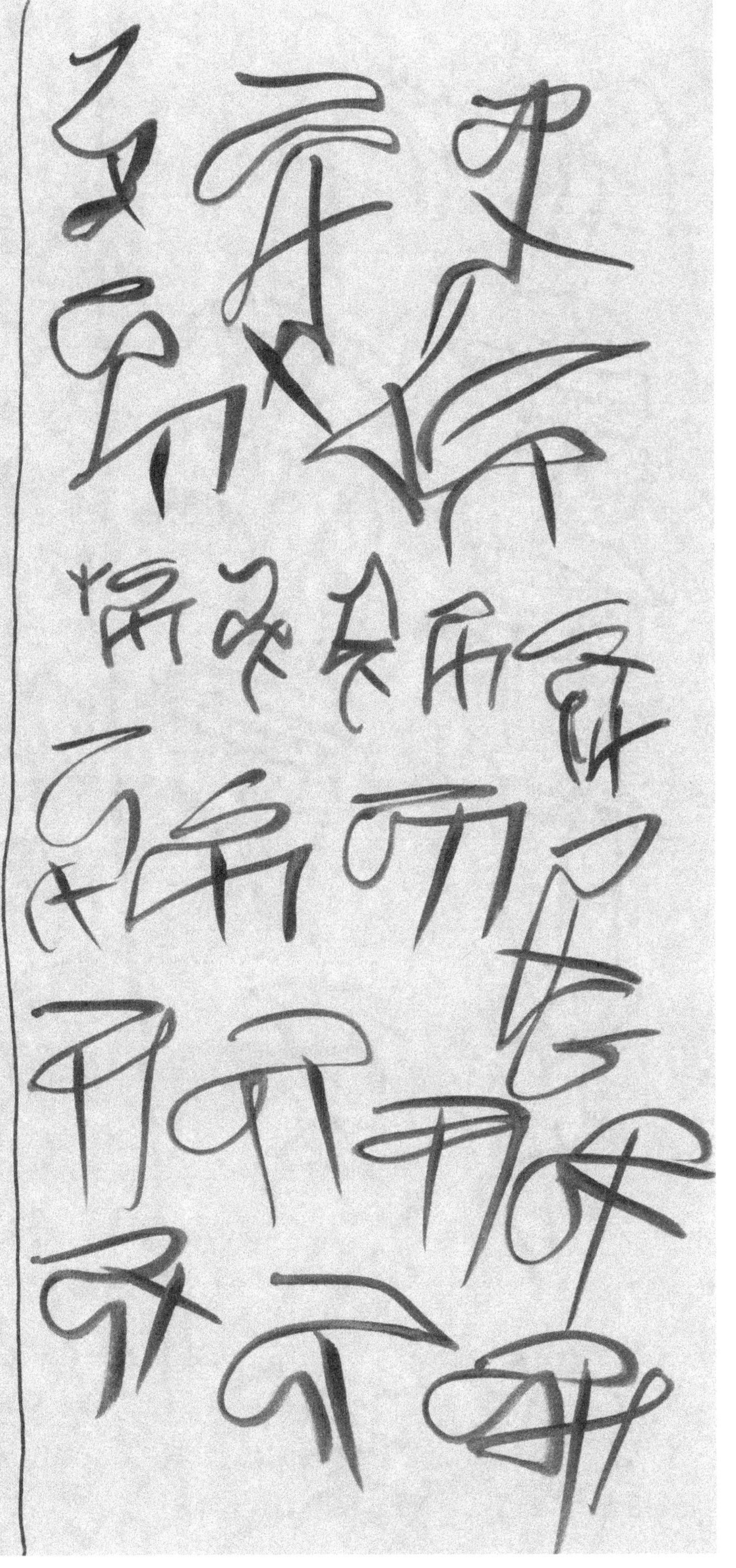

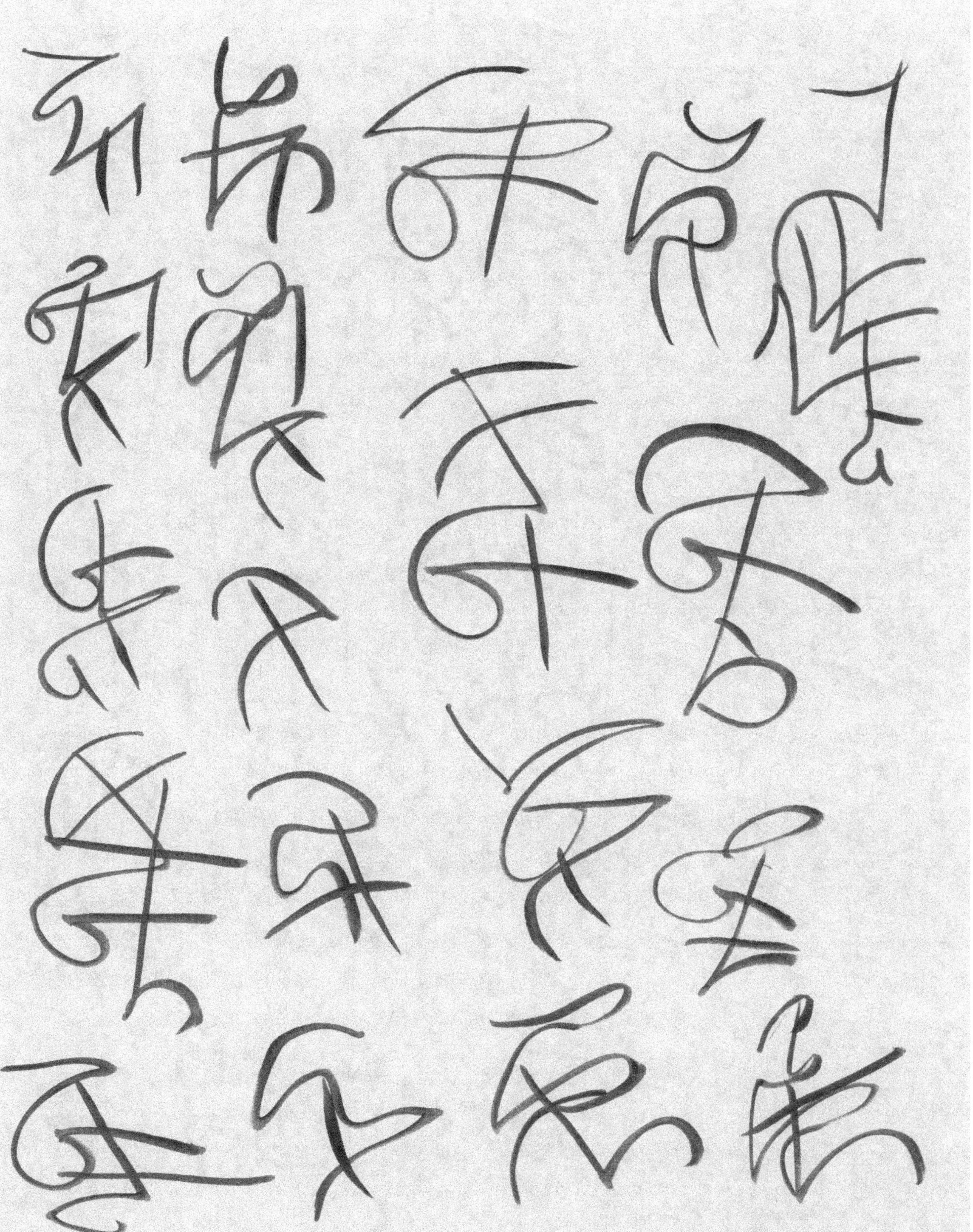

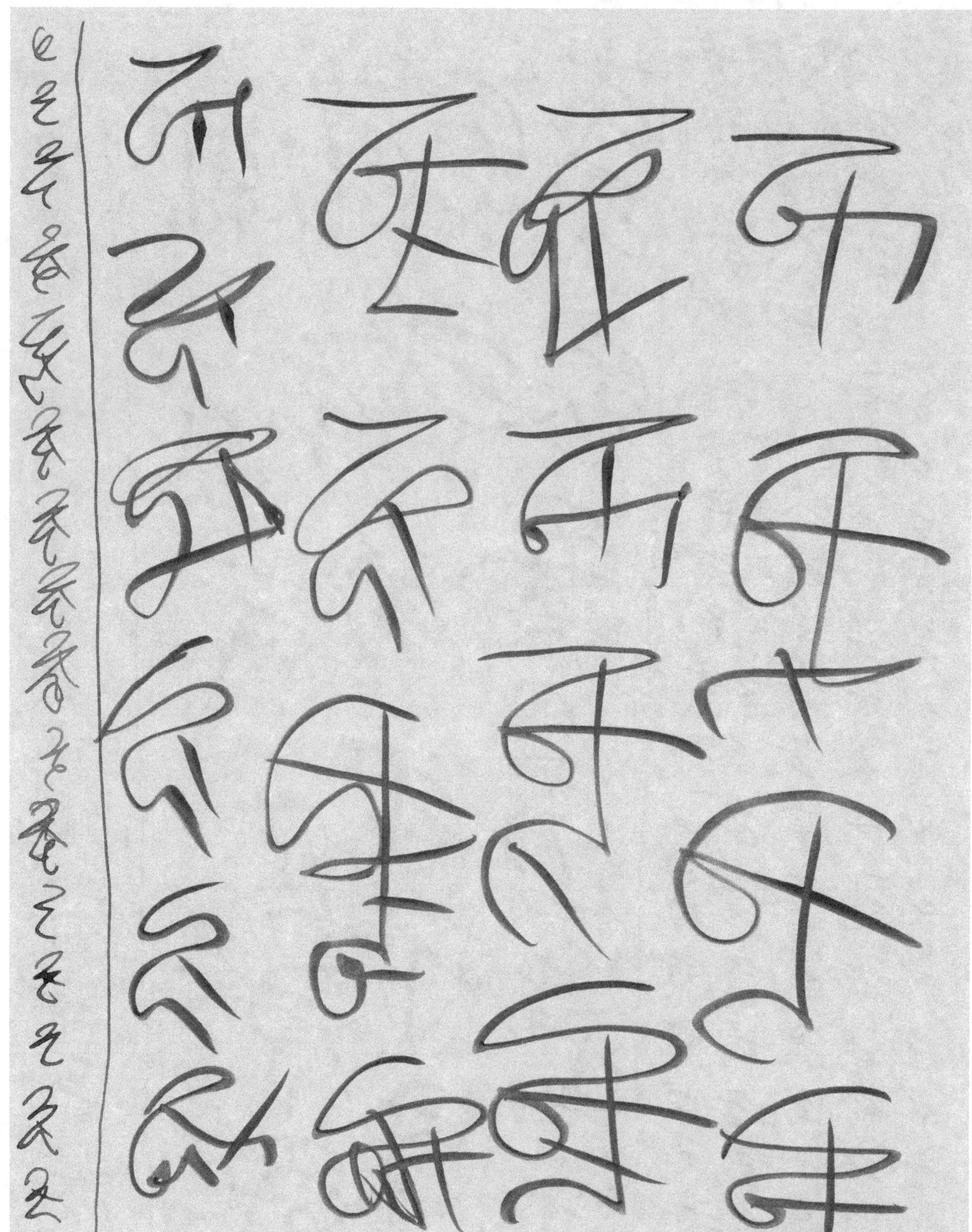

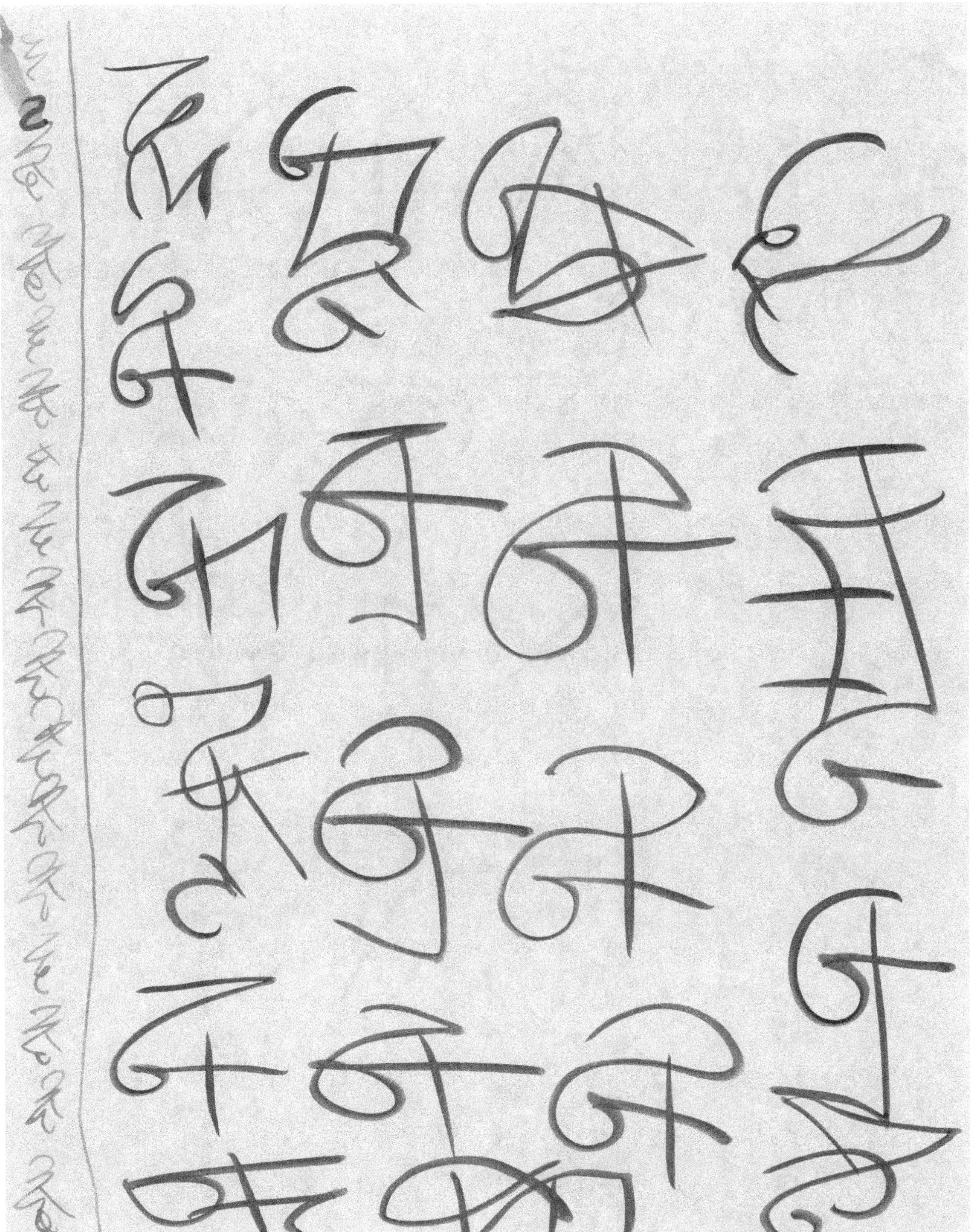

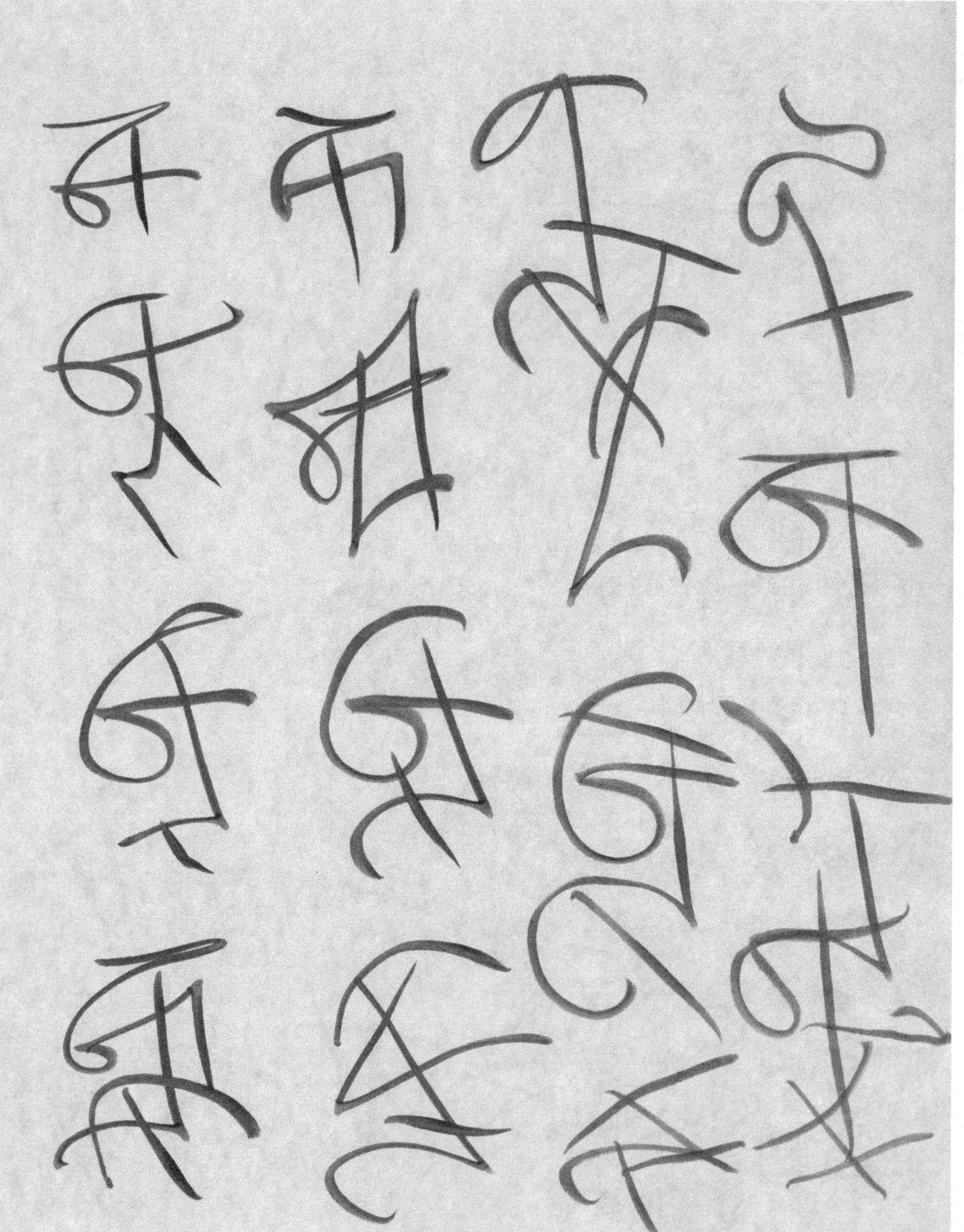

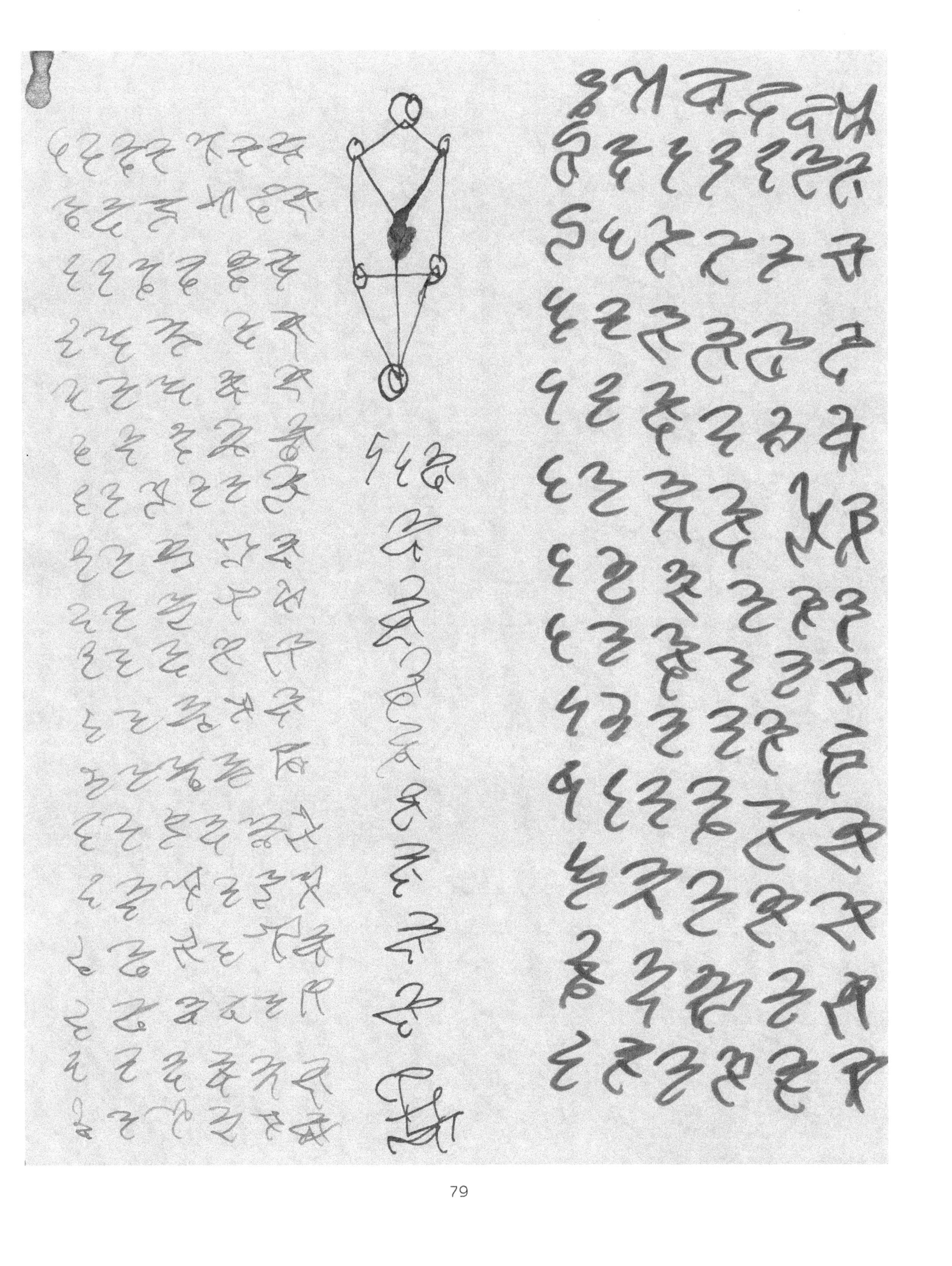

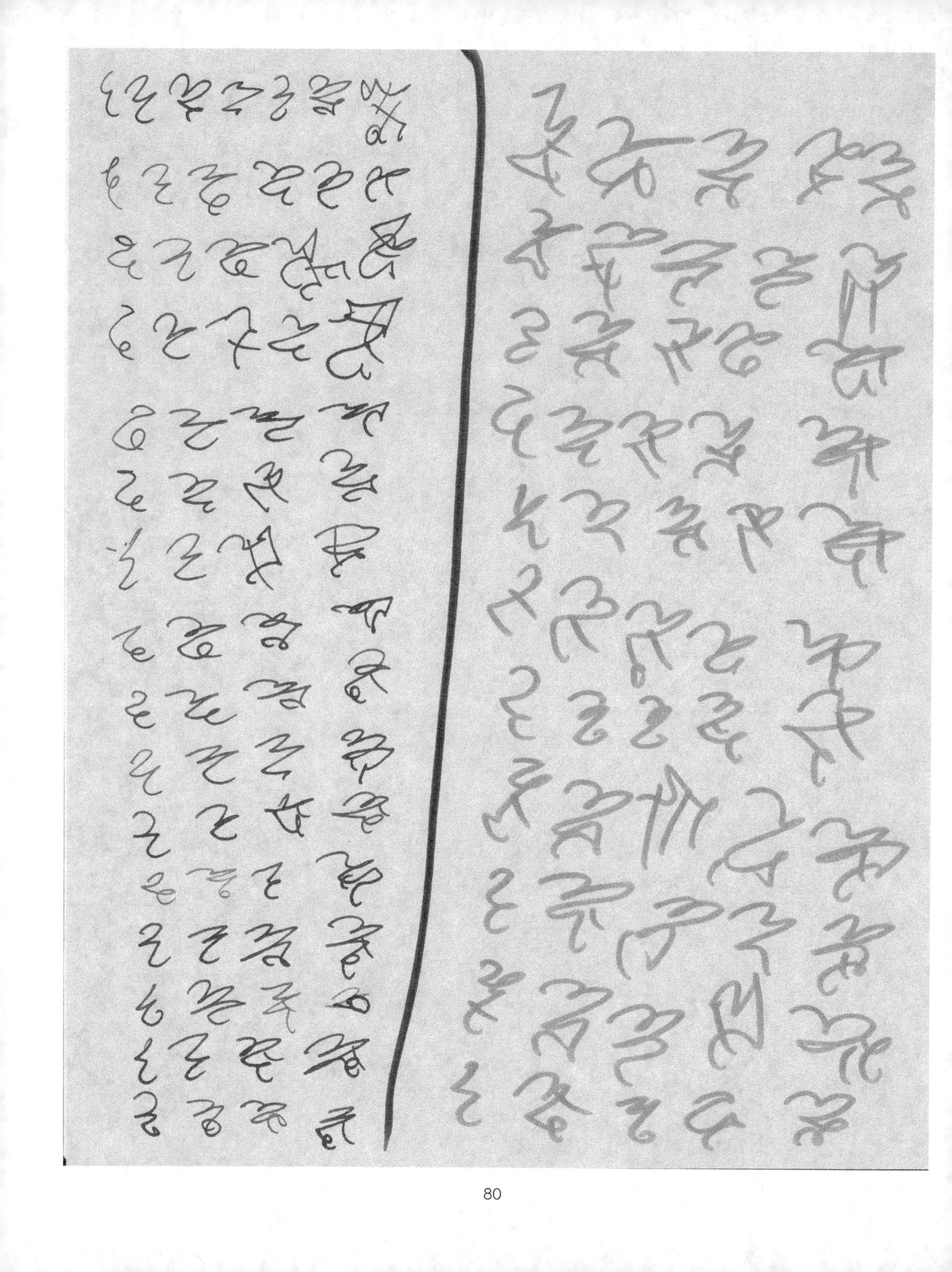

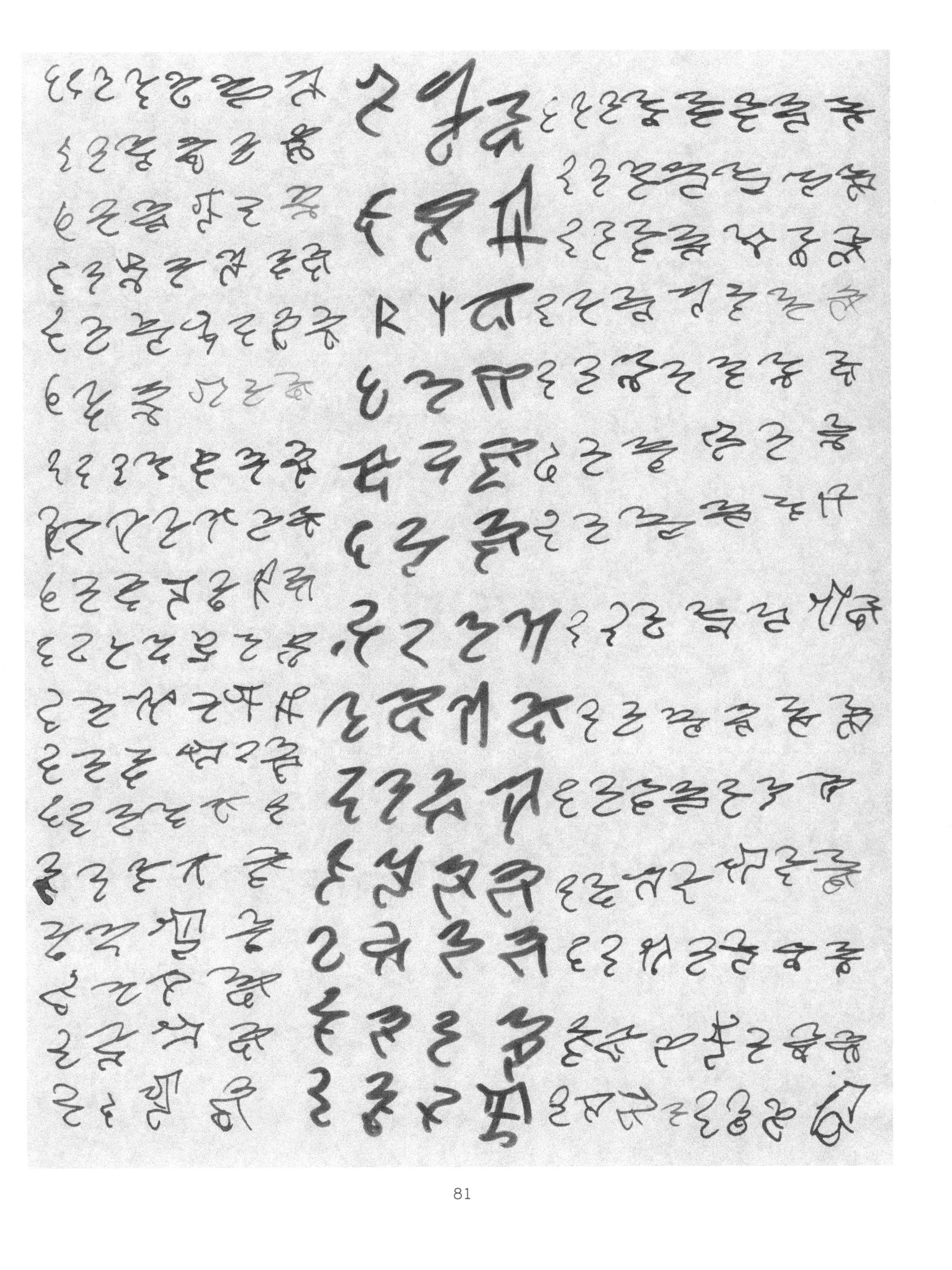

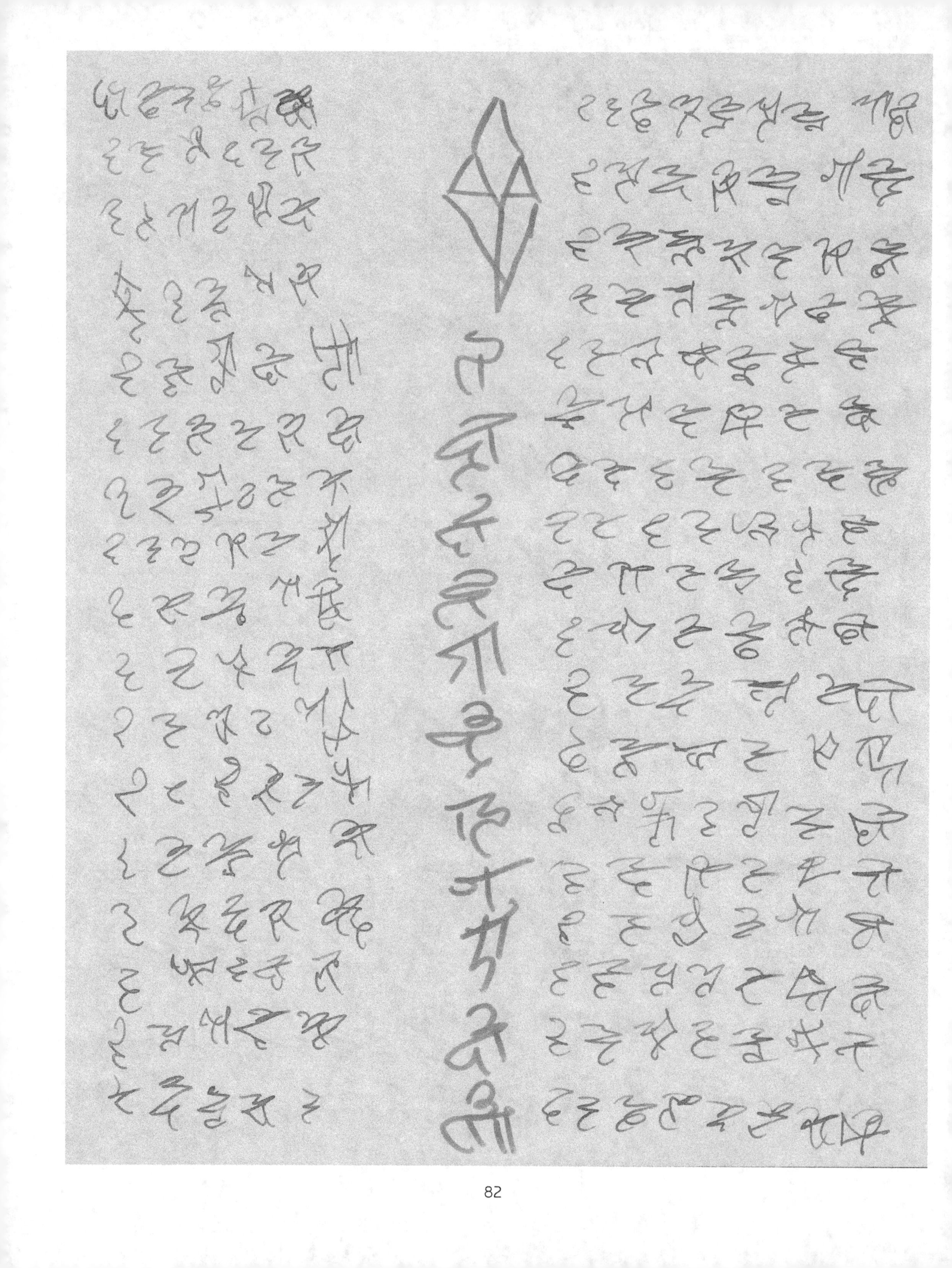

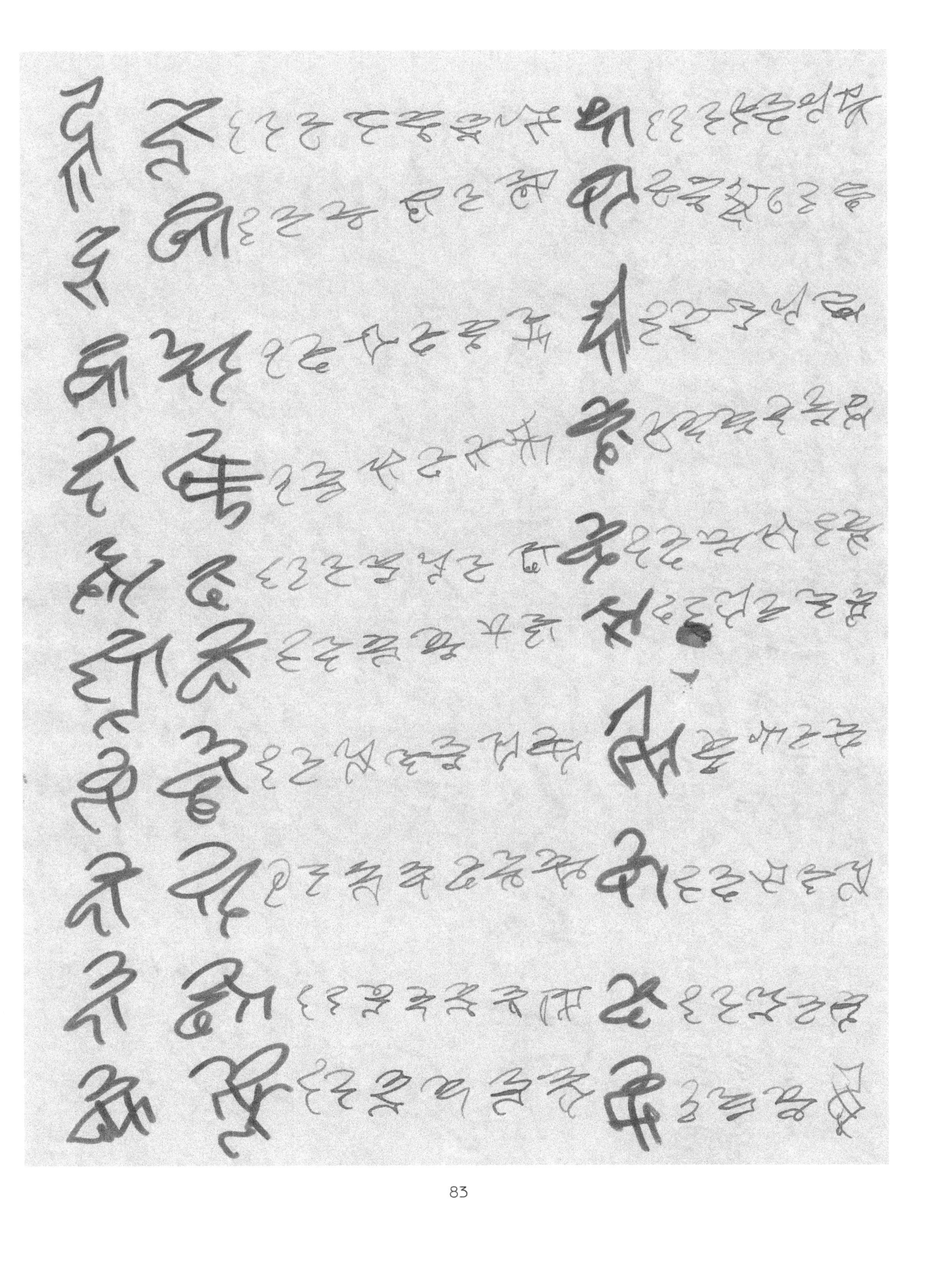

9 798890 272553